Arco Literary Critiques

Of recent years, the ordinary man who reads for pleasure has been gradually excluded from that great debate in which every intelligent reader of the classics takes part. There are two reasons for this: first, so much criticism floods from the world's presses that no one but a scholar living entirely among books can hope to read it all; and second, the critics and analysts, mostly academics, use a language that only their fellows in the same discipline can understand.

Consequently criticism, which should be as 'inevitable as breathing'—an activity for which we are all qualified—has become the private field of a few warring factions who shout their unintelligible battle cries to each other but make little communication to the common man.

Arco Literary Critiques aims at giving a straightforward account of literature and of writers—straightforward both in content and in language. Critical jargon is as far as possible avoided; any terms that must be used are explained simply; and the constant preoccupation of the authors of the Series is to be lucid.

It is our hope that each book will be easily understood, that it will adequately describe its subject without pretentiousness so that the intelligent reader who wants to know about Donne or Keats or Shakespeare will find enough in it to bring him up to date on critical estimates.

Even those who are well read, we believe, can benefit from a lucid exposition of what they may have taken for granted, and perhaps—dare it be said?—not fully understood.

K. H. G.

Between the Figures of Adam & Eve appears a fiery Gulph descending
from the Sea of fire Before the throne in this Cataract Four Angels
Descend headlong with four trumpets to awake the dead. beneath
these is the Seat of the Harlot named Mystery in the Revelations. She is
seized by Two Beings each with three heads they Represent Vegetative
Existence. as it is written in Revelations they strip her naked & burn her with
fire. beneath her feet is a flaming Cavern in which is seen
the Great Red Dragon with seven heads & ten Horns who is bound in
Chains by Two Strong Demons they are Gog & Magog. The Graves beneath
are opend & the dead awake & obey the call of the Trumpet those on the
Right hand awake in joy those on the Left in Horror. beneath the Dragons
Cavern a Skeleton begins to Animate starting into life at the Trumpets
sound while the Wicked contend with each other on the brink of

A typical page from Blake's *Notebook* (B.M. Additional 49460)

ARCO
Literary Critiques

Blake

Stanley Gardner

New York

Written for Ruth

Acknowledgements

The author and publishers are indebted to the Syndics of
the Fitzwilliam Museum, Cambridge, for permission to
reproduce the portrait of Blake by John Linnell on the
cover, and to the Trustees of the British Museum for permission to reproduce from Blake's *Notebook*, from the
manuscript of *Vala, or The Four Zoas* and from the *Songs
of Innocence*.

Published 1969 by ARCO PUBLISHING COMPANY, Inc.
219 Park Avenue South, New York, N.Y. 10003
Copyright © Stanley Gardner, 1968, 1969
All Rights Reserved
Library of Congress Catalog Number 74-78851
Printed in the United States of America

Blake

Some men, created for destruction, come
Into the world and make the world their home.
Be they as vile and base as e'er they can,
They'll still be called, 'The world's honest man'.

His writing was neglected in his lifetime, ignored or misunderstood for a hundred years and thought insane by some critics even
thirty years ago. Now he is accepted as a major poet. The transformation is unique in its extent and tardiness. No other poet
now speaks so directly to our generation about spiritual power
and personal liberty, the corruption of war and the vision of
peace. At last we have come to understand Blake, not by virtue
of clear-sightedness, but simply because time has rolled back the
evils that appalled him. We are left, however, with continuing
self-deceptions by reading into Blake's poetry what we are pleased
to hear.

This book is taken up wholly with the poetry, and with
relating it to the London that stimulated so much of it. Little
mention can be made in a book of this length of Blake's three
final works, and the commentary is mainly confined to his writing before 1794. This is most of the poetry of indisputable
greatness. Many readers have stopped at *Songs of Innocence and of
Experience* and a few other lyrics. But there is now no reason
why the Lambeth Books should not be generally read, and they
are dealt with here at some length. The reader whose resilience
is equal to tackling the final prophecies is referred to Chapter 9
and the reading list. Help is available in bulk, but the intellectual
going is precipitous.

A word is needed on Blake's illustrations, which are not mentioned later. They were once considered, perhaps out of piety, as essential to an understanding of the poetry, being 'of the same creative impulse', unless the 'verse became a mere accompaniment of his pictorial art'. None of this is true. Blake himself set the priorities in 1818 when he wrote to Dawson Turner that his illustrations, 'when printed perfect, accompany poetical personifications and acts, without which poems they could never have been executed'. And far from being 'of the same creative impulse', sometimes years elapsed between the writing and illustrating of a poem. For instance, when he was illustrating *Songs of Innocence* Blake was writing or had written the 'contrary' *Songs of Experience*. Furthermore, many illustrations refer only to a few lines of text, or even to a different page of text altogether. In brief, we are left with the poetry to radiate its own meaning.

S. G.

Contents

The Author

Stanley Gardner, who is Headmaster of Wanstead High School, gained an international literary award in New York with his first book on Blake. He has also edited Keats's *Selected Letters*, Dryden's *Selected Poems* and a number of Shakespeare's plays, and is General Editor of the *New Warwick Shakespeare*.

A page from Blake's manuscript of *Vala, or The Four Zoas*, 1797 (B.M. Additional 39764). The poem was not published in Blake's lifetime

I

Introduction

Do not lean out of the window

Most of us have seen that warning in a railway carriage, and the association of these words with railway carriages is so strong that the recollection is immediate and irresistible. And the dominance of this recollection determines the meaning of the word 'window' when it appears at the end of this particular sentence. It means a pane of glass set in a stout frame in a railway carriage door, and movable by means of a strap with holes in it. The definition is precise. Our minds not only exclude from the sentence all other panes of glass outside the carriage, but we know too that the application of the warning to any window other than one inside the carriage is absurd. There is nothing explicit in the sentence to tell us this; the meaning is implicit, and our reaction to it is immediate, indeed almost intuitive.

If we change the sentence very slightly the whole situation is transformed:

Lean out of the window, Goldenhair

Now the letters that spell 'window' have nothing to do with railway carriages, unless the speaker is twirling a moustache. The movement of the line is part of its meaning, and makes it romantic. 'Goldenhair' is evocative; she (what has determined the sex?) is of ideal proportions, age and aspect. The word 'window' has probably not raised in our minds the thought of glass at all. It is important now not as a barrier but as a means of access. Our imagination, always ready to yearn and sigh, leaps at the easy romantic chance, and loads the word with atmosphere—flowers, warm evenings, balconies. The window may be in a country house or a lodge. It may be in Cornwall or Spain or the South of France; but it is not in a boiler-house or a betting shop or a laundry. But why not? Now, too, the word 'lean' is strangely altered. In this second sentence the implications of the word are subtly but extensively elaborated. The dictionary meaning may be the same in both sentences; but not the meaning for the writer or the reader.

If we put the sentence back into the negative we change the meaning yet again:

Do not lean out of the window, Goldenhair

The word 'lean' is no longer suffused with romantic purpose, and the window, no longer a means of communication, has become once again a barrier—perhaps and perhaps not in a railway carriage. The direct association with the railway is dispelled by the last word. Yet location is utterly changed, and may or may not now be in a boiler-house or a betting shop or a laundry. The simple restitution of the negative has broken down at once the facile poetic effect. It has knocked at least a decade off the age of Goldenhair and deprived her of all sensual relevance. In the first sentence we quoted, the speaker (or writer) was quite impersonal, in the second the speaker was an idealised presence with whom the reader was expected to identify himself, but in the third sentence the person speaking is immediately present. We sense a much more direct relationship between the speaker and the person addressed.

Even for a sentence as simple as this the reactions of the reader are complex. But this familiar word 'window' can be charged much more powerfully than we have experienced so far:

Five windows light the caverned man. Through one he breathes the air,
Through one hears music of the spheres. Through one the Eternal Vine
Flourishes, that he may receive the grapes. Through one can look
And see small portions of the Eternal World that ever groweth.

Through one pass out what time he please, but he will not,
For stolen joys are sweet and bread eaten in secret pleasant.

EUROPE, Introduction 1–6

At once the reader knows that none of the meanings we have already seen represented by the word is relevant here. At the same time, though the lines are not obviously 'poetic' in the conventional sense of the word, as was our sentence about Goldenhair, they are clearly much more effective poetry. At once we know that the five windows represent the five senses. But this is only the beginning, only the merest hint of the full poetic meaning of the word as the passage develops its powerful and ultimately disturbing theme. And through using the simple link between the abstract senses and the five windows Blake makes us experience the inadequacy of our moral preconceptions. To be sure, we can restate in paraphrase what Blake says. But the restatement will be like looking at a black and white photograph, whereas the way Blake says it we are walking through his landscape. The greater the poetry, very often the more difficult it is to define a word. The poet relies upon its ambiguity for his meaning. Clearly Blake is concerned with certain functions of the window which we understand from the idea he is conveying to us and which change as the context develops. The material existence of the window is of little significance, indeed hardly enters the mind. The intellectual quality of the propositions is compelling, and excludes it. And by not defining the word precisely the poet directs our imagination through a series of associative meanings. As the associated ideas extend and reverberate, our imagination is dramatically committed to realising the stress, conflict, anger, delight, incredulity—whatever it is that has compelled the poet to write. It is the refusal of the word to be limited to a simple definition that allows this creative process to work.

ii

Looking back at our four uses of the word 'window' we find that when the word can be most closely defined, the emotional charge is lowest. In the first sentence British Rail express no emotion at all; they are not even moved to threaten a fine. We know precisely what the window is, and the word 'lean' represents a simple straightforward action uncomplicated by overtones. Here language is used the way scientists or lawyers might use it. Good English here is precise. A word represents one single concept. So when a scientist speaks of 'velocity' he does not mean 'speed'. 'Weight' is one thing, 'mass' is another. The words are clearly defined and are used as signs, with the same precise reference as is applied to such signs as π or r or $=$. A scientist requires one word to have one meaning for the sake of clarity and convenience. But words do not conform to this pattern easily. For instance, mass for the physicist is not weight; but he is hard put to it to sustain the distinction into the adjective 'massive'. By then the word has escaped.

Here we see a word slipping the handcuffs of a definition. Or, to put it another way, language has a natural and inevitable tendency towards poetry. And this tendency is stimulated once emotions or human relationships are involved. So in our second sentence with the word 'window', once Goldenhair comes into the reckoning to arouse emotions and relationships, however trite and threadbare, the window escapes definition to give imagination scope. And with it goes the word 'lean'. The process is cumulative, generating a natural momentum. It is the defined state that is artificial.

So, once the word 'lean' escapes from the definition imposed upon it in the railway notice, it acquires a symbolic meaning from its poetic context:

Lean out of the window, Goldenhair

Now it is charged with implications. The lady is not invited to lean out of the window for the good of her health or because the day is bright. The movement of the line tells us that the invitation is hopefully romantic; if she leans, the action will symbolise at least her interest in the speaker, at best her ultimate devotion. The action 'lean' symbolises a frame of mind, a relationship, something intangible and inexpressible. This is something quite different from the scientific use of words as signs—mass, velocity and so forth.

The reader may recollect the clause on page 9, 'unless the speaker is twirling a moustache'. This action was clearly intended to symbolise villainy, and comprehension of this fact in the reader depends upon the recollection of the familiar villains of Victorian melodrama. If the reader has no knowledge of such melodramatic villains, the point is lost, because he cannot possibly make the association of the percept (the symbolic act—twirling a moustache) with the concept (the abstract idea—villainy). This leads us to what is probably the most important requirement of a symbol—that it must be familiarly recognisable. So a poet who wishes to use symbols must either use those already established in the reader's experience, or he must create his own symbolism by associating certain percepts repeatedly with certain concepts until recognition is established.

We notice also how the mention of the moustache-twirling on page 9 momentarily altered the significance of the window: there was a fleeting recognition that 'window' was related to danger. So again a symbol is influenced by, and influences, the words around it. This is quite different from the behaviour of a word (e.g. velocity, mass) used as a sign in good logical English, and is the natural behaviour of language.

One final point: say I had written, 'unless the speaker is twirling a *villainous* moustache'. The unnecessary explanation dissipates the effect; it sounds arch, and is unworthy of the reader. So the writer, especially the poet, has to take a chance, because the recognition has to be in a way intuitive. Whether the effect is humorous or tragic, it still has to be disturbing; explanation reduces the disturbance.

However, this sort of explanatory adjective, which confirms the primary meaning of a symbol, is quite different from a qualification that develops the meaning. As we saw, a symbol (like all words in poetry) lives upon its context.

So Blake hints at the symbol of the sun in this Song of Innocence, the opening lines of *The Echoing Green*:

The sun does arise
And make happy the skies;
The merry bells ring
To welcome the spring.

Elsewhere he writes:

He who binds to himself a joy
Does the winged life destroy,
But he who kisses the joy as it flies
Lives in Eternity's sun-rise.

ETERNITY

Primarily the sun is a symbol of joy and divine love. But gradually this is overwhelmed by lust, avarice, tyranny and malice till the terrible time in Experience when

The sun arises in the east,
Clothed in robes of blood and gold;
Swords and spears and wrath increased
All around his bosom rolled,
Crowned with warlike fires and raging desires.

DAY

The percept (the thing perceived), the sun, is qualified till it takes on a changed, and here tragic, force. The rhythm of the poem, the pontifical beginning, an impressive processional, collapsing into the ungovernable rout at the end, is part of the meaning. The grammar of the sentence breaks down under the stress. But then, grammar is the logic of language and is irrelevant to poetry. Poetry is not logical. It is natural.

Most of our time is spent in relationship, one way or another, with other people. Conflicts and tensions develop, and grammar breaks down. And continually from day to day, as emotion or drama, however insignificant, involves us, the language we use moves away from strict definition. We begin to use figures of speech, or to speak in symbols. The difference between 'go to the devil' and 'please depart' is that the former expresses our anger as well as our request. 'Gale, force nine' is a definition used by meteorologists, and means a strong gale to a reader who knows the code. 'That wind would blow your hair off' means more, and something rather different—a frame of mind generated after encountering a gale, force nine. And everyone understands it.

At once we appreciate that 'go to the devil' and 'that wind would blow your hair off' are less scientifically precise than 'please depart' and 'gale, force nine'. They are also more poetic, more charged with feeling. They are also the words we should be more likely to use in the circumstances envisaged. So we use figurative language and symbols every day. It is commonplace. We expect words to break out, to say more than the dictionary gives them credit for. We may not speak great poetry every hour we live, but we habitually lace our speech with poetic phrases, trite or spontaneous, inspired or hackneyed, and there is a clear and natural link between spoken language and poetry. And just as we expect our listener to understand and appreciate our mood when we speak out forcefully, so poetry must convey its meaning, not conceal it. It may be difficult, but should not be obscure. Blake's poetry, like most great poetry, is difficult and tough; it is not obscure, until he ceases to write poetry.

iii

We have all seen the business letter that goes: 'We are in receipt of your esteemed order of 17th ult.... assuring you of our prompt attention at all times . . . We have the honour . . . humble servants . . .'

This prose is written to conceal as well as to convey meaning. It gives the writer a deferential anonymity. The order has probably not been 'esteemed' at all; yet convention demands that this be said. 'Prompt attention' may well be more real in the assurance than in fact. The writer is probably quite unconscious of the honour he is 'having', and his humility is unlikely.

The phrases in which the letter is set relax the reader. They are recognisable, reassuring and safe. They exclude tension and put beyond question any uncomfortable relationships. The expressions of service and attention are read in the spirit in which they are written, not necessarily with expectation of fulfilment. It seems paradoxical that with its exaggerated emphasis the language simultaneously draws attention to itself and drains itself of meaning. But no one can deny that the writer is *serious*.

Let us now have a few lines from a *serious* poem:

> Behold, in Calder's vale, where wide around
> Unnumbered villas creep the shrubby hills,
> A spacious dome for this fair purpose rise.
> High o'er the open gates, with gracious air,
> Eliza's image stands. By gentle steps
> Up-raised, from room to room we slowly walk,
> And view with wonder and with silent joy
> The sprightly scene, where many a busy hand,
> Where spools, cards, wheels and looms with motion quick,
> And ever-murmuring sound, the unwonted sense
> Wrap in surprise. To see them all employed,
> All blithe, it gives the spreading heart delight,
> As neither meats, nor drinks, nor aught of joy
> Corporeal can bestow. Nor less they gain
> Virtue than wealth, while, on their useful works
> From day to day intent, in their full minds
> Evil no place can find.

THE FLEECE VII, 259–75

Those lines by John Dyer describe a visit in 1757, the year Blake was born, to a 'mansion' erected by 'the sons of trade', in which the poor and destitute were to be 'compelled to happiness'. The 'mansion' is a workhouse, then usually called a house of industry. The verses are very serious, just as the merchant's letter was serious. And their aim is much the same.

Again the language is precisely what the 18th-century reader would expect: *spacious dome, fair purpose, silent joy, sprightly scene*. The poet sees the inmates 'all employed, all blithe', he manages to express the magnanimity that swells in his own heart at the sight of the poor gainfully employed and kept from evil. He might be describing a place of pastoral delight, and the language conceals the appalling truth (if the poet sees it at all), and reassures the reader that all is well under his and God's benevolence. And important to the poet is his own gentility in mounting stairs.

This verse is serious, but it is far from great. The great poet makes us feel uncomfortable; he is not serious, but direct, as Blake was direct when he considered the frightening little mills in Spitalfields, where a room housed a loom and a family starving at their labour behind sealed windows, and where he heard

> The shuttles of death sing in the sky to Islington and Pancras,
> Round Marylebone to Tyburn's river, weaving black melancholy
>   as a net,
> And despair as meshes closely wove over the west of London.
>
> JERUSALEM, 41–3

In every age, once a reader sees a poem he anticipates both the manner and the matter of the writer before he starts. Certain words and thoughts are officially 'poetic', and others are not. The challenge comes when the poet's thoughts cannot be anticipated, and the reader is asked to hear not the consoling and 'ever-murmuring sound' of looms, but the 'shuttles of death' singing over London.

The poet's dilemma is that he can only convey his meaning within the terms of reference that his readers recognise. At the same time he must disturb these terms of reference if his poetry is to survive. Certain words and sentences have inevitable associations for readers, and certain places are associated with recognisable frames of mind. A cottage with smoke rising from the chimney is the start of a poem; a slaughter-house with smoke rising from the chimney is not. Goldenhair could never raise the thought in us that she might be leaning out of a rusty window; but she could lean out of a broken casement. Each poet, in every generation, inherits a catalogue of such confirmed responses that have a kind of official authority. It is easy to write within the catalogue, confirming the reader's preconceptions and reasserting the old truisms. It is a labour of genius to deny the preconceptions and reveal the truisms as threadbare, when all habitual thinking and expectation are working against the attempt, and the old associations circumscribe it. It seems a vicious circle impossible to break. Blake broke the circle.

2

Blake's Westminster

Time and again in his poetry Blake returns to attack the social and spiritual evils that laid waste to most of the city, and that created 'the terrible desert' of London in the 18th century. The elegance, manners and style, the music and polished conversation that we mainly associate with the times belonged to privilege only, and very few Londoners indeed were privileged. The gilded rooms of society were sustained on foundations deep in poverty and degradation. It is true that in this century men became philanthropically aware of the human misery around them, and 'humane' institutions began and flourished. But the charity was always qualified by expediency and its extent was necessarily ineffectual. And for all the endeavour, it was like shovelling sand against the tide, while the basic principle that a massive, subservient and unaspiring labour force was fundamental to commercial prosperity remained an instinctive assumption of the most enlightened social opinion.

One man alone, Blake, questioned this assumption, and all other assumptions that set man against his neighbour. He never compromised. He withdrew as he grew old into a landscape of obscure, almost impenetrable mythology, but (unlike Wordsworth) he still refused to come to terms. He would make none of the concessions to expedience that are essential in a successful social reformer, and knew nothing of the politic art of what is possible. For him the motives of charity made charity sickening:

Compel the poor to live upon a crust of bread, by soft mild arts.
Smile when they frown, frown when they smile; and when a man looks pale
With labour and abstinence, say he looks healthy and happy.
And when his children sicken, let them die. There are enough
Born, even too many, and our earth will be overrun
Without these arts. If you will make the poor live with temperance,
With pomp give every crust of bread you give—with gracious cunning
Magnify small gifts. Reduce a man to want a gift, and then give with pomp.

THE FOUR ZOAS VII, a

Blake attacked the dogma that God created rich and poor, master and servant. The churches and their teaching were for him mills of oppression and a bible of hypocrisy, a pontifical denial of Christ. Until a transformation was accepted at the very heart of the matter, Jerusalem was beyond recall, and London would remain a place where

> . . . souls of men are bought and sold
> And milk-fed infancy for gold;
> And youth to slaughter-houses led,
> And beauty for a bit of bread.

THE HUMAN IMAGE

ii

Blake's father was a hosier in a fair way of business at 28 Broad Street, where William was born on November 28, 1757. The house, now 74 Broadwick Street, still stands, a little to the south-east of what is now Oxford Circus.

Blake lived here, or near here, until he moved to Lambeth in 1793, and the vicinity shaped his whole imagination.

In the late 18th century Oxford Street's ominous old name of Tyburn Road was still a recent memory, and Regent Street did not exist. Broad Street itself had seen better days. The well-to-do householders for whom the street was built earlier in the century had moved out, and the street was occupied in the main by

19

people in a small way of business, some of the houses being divided into lodgings.

Round the corner from Blake's house was Carnaby Market, 'built on a piece of ground called the Pest-field'. The market included a slaughter-house, with women among its butchers, and the voices of the cattle he heard brought in for slaughter stayed with Blake all his life.

28 Broad Street was built on a piece of land known as Pest-house Close, and it was only some twenty years before Blake was born that the pesthouse was moved away from Westminster to Paddington—'mournful ever-weeping Paddington' Blake called it. Indeed, it was opening up Pesthouse Close that enabled the house to be built. Most of Pesthouse Close was by that time built over with mean houses, but part of the area was used as an extension to the adjacent burial ground on land called Pawlett's Garden. In the Pawlett's Garden burial ground was the St. James's Workhouse, 'capable of containing 300 poor people. When any of the poor fall sick, they are removed to the infirmary, which is in a street called the Gravel Pits near Broad Street.' After 1789 the burial ground in Pawlett's Garden and in Pesthouse Close was incorporated into the workhouse enclosure, and the parish acquired a new burial ground beside the Hampstead Road in St. Pancras. In any case, neither the Garden nor the Close could accommodate any more dead.

The conditions in the workhouse were appalling. In 1741 it was reported: 'the stench hardly supportable, poor creatures almost naked and the living go to bed to the dead.' The inmates were strictly controlled, allowed out after service on Sundays, and put to tasks of weaving, spinning and the like during the hours of daylight.

In 1782 the parish overseers of the poor took over an old riding school in King Street (now Kingly Street) hardly a hundred yards west of Blake's home, and equipped it as a School of Industry for older children from the workhouse. Part of the building was still used as stables. Both boys and girls were admitted, and after strict training and regular religious discipline the boys were sent to sea or apprenticed, and the girls 'placed out in service'.

Other poor boys were trained in a charity school situated above the watch house by St. James's Church, until the boys and the constables were both moved to Little Vine Street.

If Blake came out of his front door and walked a few yards south down Marshall Street he came to Golden Square, 'which is very small, but neat, and is adorned on the inside with grass plats and gravel walks, and is surrounded with handsome iron rails'. In the middle was a statue, claimed to be of George III. There was, in fact, a monarch surveying almost every square.

This was a different world from Pesthouse Close, where the grave-maker offended his neighbours by pulling up and burning in his house the 'old rotten coffin boards' until the law stopped him. Here in Golden Square, so near in space to the workhouse, so distant in status, lived a cosmopolitan gentry. From time to time the square housed baronets, peers, peeresses, generals, various artists and miniaturists, English and foreign, writers, people in professions and business, surgeons and tradesmen. Only the very highest ranking people had by the second half of the century moved away from Golden Square nearer to St. James's. Golden Square with its lamplit lawn and smooth gravel remained a vivid translation from the degradation a little to the north beyond Broad Street.

At times the foreign legations moved into Golden Square, and indeed the whole area had an unconventional air. Some streets were 'much inhabited by the French', who had their places of worship, as did Anabaptists, Presbyterians, and Independents.

Dominating all this was royalty and the church. Indeed, as Blake walked towards the south-west of the parish, he made as it were a symbolic journey across the social landscape of the 18th century. Opposite the parish church of St. James, Piccadilly, the young and extravagant Lord Melbourne had built his mansion, now called Albany; he and Lady Melbourne took possession in 1774, though the stables had been occupied, in the architect's revealing phrase, by 'the Cattle, as horses, grooms and coach-men' for a twelvemonth. Melbourne's mistress told a friend that the house and furnishings 'would cost him one hundred thousand pounds'. Against this, the eleven hundred paupers in the parish cost about £6,000 a year. The ducal families of St. James's could look out of their broad windows and relax in the solace that hardship was a divine dispensation, and that 'the many noble structures, which have of late arisen for the relief of maladies and miseries of every species, have been justly quoted as proofs of our public humanity'.

Moreover, the inevitable perpetuation of servile poverty was not only essential to the well-being of the affluent, but a benefit in eternity to the labourers on earth. All knew the lesson that the poor were dear to the Lord, and that their reward was promised, as Blake said, in 'an allegorical abode where existence hath never come'.

In 1791 Melbourne turned Albany over to Frederick, Duke of York. An earlier Duke of York, later James II, was revealingly involved with the beginnings of the parish church. It was consecrated in 1684, and 'was dedicated to St. James, in compliment to the name of the Duke of York'. Here Blake was baptised, and the church, dedicated to a saint in deference to a duke, epitomised in a politely cynical way the unanswerable alliance between Crown and Church that Blake saw as a conspiracy of brutal hypocrisy.

It seems to me that too much has been made in the past of other influences on Blake's poetry. All else seems to me academic beside his quite crucial reactions to the commonplace misery and arrogance that hung in the air he breathed.

Particularly unrewarding too is speculation on the happiness or otherwise of Blake's childhood. His parents are said to have failed to comprehend him, and much has been made of relating the tyrannical father-figure that recurs in his poetry to Blake's own childhood. He is said to have rebelled and withdrawn into childish visions, and again the evidence for this is often read into his poetry. The point is of critical interest, because it has been held that when Blake wrote against the alliance of parental and religious authority he was recollecting his own childhood. The evidence for this assumption is slight. The impulse of Blake's poetry did not lie in autobiographical recollection. I can see no analogy at all with Wordsworth's recollections of the 'intimations of immortality' he had as a boy.

iii

Because, it is said, he 'so hated a blow', Blake's father spared his son the rigours and tedium of conventional schooling and sent him in 1768 to Pars's Drawing School in the Strand.

In August 1772 Blake was apprenticed to James Basire, and for the next five years spent much time, often in Westminster Abbey, making drawings for the Society of Antiquaries, to whom Basire was engraver. In this work Blake found 'a treasure which he knew how to value . . . unentangled in the intricate mazes of modern practice'. His earliest original engraving, 'Joseph of Arimathaea among the Rocks of Albion', is dated 1773 and inscribed, strangely for a boy of sixteen: 'This is one of the Gothic artists who built the cathedrals in what we call the dark ages, wandering around in sheepskins and goatskins, of whom the world was not worthy; such were the Christians in all ages.'

As Blake reported years later to George Cumberland, one of the founders of the National Gallery, and Blake's friend to the end of his life: 'I myself remember when I thought my pursuits in art a kind of criminal dissipation and neglect of the main chance, which I hid my face for not being able to abandon as a passion which is forbidden by law and religion.' The sense of following a calling not encouraged by his elders and the long periods in the Abbey combined to give Blake a training in solitary independence as complete and thorough as his training in drawing. Both lasted all his life.

But if his training in drawing was prolonged and complete, it was his only formal education. He escaped entirely the commonplace instruction in the classics and Latin grammar, and was never put through the conventional course in English versification. So his grammar was always wholesomely English, unaffected by Latin 'correctness', and he was not well-bred in poetic good manners. No reading was prescribed for him, and the conventional standards of taste were never forced in his mind. He read of his own choice Milton, Shakespeare and Spenser and knew his contemporary poets; among philosophers he had read Burke, Locke and Bacon, 'with contempt and abhorrence'.

Again, it is as if the reading were devised to breed independence. It is difficult to match these philosophers with solitary days on end in Westminster Abbey. There was no one to challenge him to accept or refute these philosophies dialectically, and Blake responded with his imagination rather than his reason. He disliked these works because, he said, 'they mock inspiration and vision. Inspiration and vision was then, and now is, and I hope will always remain, my element, my eternal dwelling place'.

Blake's upbringing and training unintentionally fostered his inclination to test everything—social injustice, morality, private inhibitions, civil authority, religion, the rights of man and, later, *The Rights of Man*—not against an intellectual yardstick but in the light of his imagination. So he did not become a poet with a message, but a poet with a vision. His cry was not to reform but to recreate.

When he was twenty-one Blake became for a short time a student in the newly-established Royal Academy, but he was, as always, a difficult pupil, and was soon telling G. M. Moser, the Keeper, that he knew neither the beginning nor the end of art. Blake was furious that Reynolds should have recommended him 'to work with less extravagance and more simplicity, and to correct his drawing'. This was 'an affront never to be forgotten'.

So Blake's refusal to compromise, which is his unique strength in the face of injustice and hypocrisy and gives his poetry the 'peculiar honesty' that Eliot saw in all great poetry—this uncompromising independence shifts into obstinate wrong-headedness when seen from some angles. And again, his training as a painter and his reactions to the training seem to foster not only his qualities but his defects as a poet. His certainty in his own vision not only made him resent criticism as intrusion, but also deprived him of self-criticism. So in later life he came to conduct an obsessive and bewildering dialogue with the powers and demons of his visionary imagination.

iv

Henry Chamberlain of Hatton Garden two years later told how 'the year 1768 began with a very severe frost, which greatly contributed to the calamity of the lower sort of people, who were already severely distressed by the exorbitant price of provisions'.

On March 16, John Wilkes failed to get into Parliament to represent the City. But 'he seemed to be the darling of the populace' who, 'to show their zeal, took the horses from his carriage and drew it themselves', and at nine o'clock on March 28, 'in the middle of Brentford Butts', John Wilkes was elected by his 'friends to liberty'.

At night 'the rabble were very tumultuous. Some persons who had voted in favour of Mr. Wilkes having put out lights, the mob paraded the whole town from east to west, obliging everybody to illuminate and breaking the windows of such as did not do it immediately. The windows of the Mansion House in particular were demolished all to pieces, together with a large chandelier and some pier glasses, to the amount of many hundred pounds. In short the whole evening was one continued scene of noise and tumult'.

The next day orders were given to the guards on duty at St. James's to be in readiness at the beat of a drum.

While the coal-heavers of Wapping fought a series of pitched and ferocious battles because 'the undertakers got fortunes, while they who did the work were starving', and were paid only 'in liquor and goods of a bad quality' instead of wages, John Wilkes faced indictment for republishing the *North Briton*. Wilkes claimed the criticism of the King's ministers in the paper to be true—it 'brings very heavy charges home to them'.

25

The city was in ferment. Two battalions of the guards lay at arms in St. James's Park and in St. George's Fields, and those at St. James's, the Savoy and the Tower 'were all kept in readiness to march at a minute's warning'. Despite this, on April 27 when Wilkes, having been refused bail, was 'being conveyed to the King's Bench Prison in a hackney coach . . . the mob stopped the coach on Westminster Bridge, took out the horses, drew it along the Strand, Fleet Street, etc. to Spitalfields. When they came to Spital Square they obliged the two tipstaffs to get out and let them go very quietly away. They then drew Mr. Wilkes to the Three Tuns Tavern in Spitalfields, where from a one pair of stairs window he earnestly entreated them to retire, which they did accordingly. After which he went in a private manner and surrendered himself to the marshal of the King's Bench Prison'.

From prison Wilkes wrote to his freeholders in Middlesex: 'Under all the oppressions which ministerial rage and revenge can invent, my steady purpose is to concert with you and other true friends of this country, the most probable means of rooting out the remains of arbitrary power and star chamber inquisition, and of improving as well as securing the generous plans of freedom, which were the boasts of our ancestors, and I trust will remain the noblest inheritance of our posterity, the only genuine characteristic of Englishmen.'

Besides the coal-heavers, the seamen were in riotous mood. While Wilkes was in prison, thousands marched on St. James's from St. George's Fields, 'with colours flying, drums beating and fifes playing'. On May 11 fifteen thousand seamen marched on Westminster demanding higher wages, and after 'they were addressed by two gentlemen, mounted on the roof of a hackney coach . . . matters were accommodated to their general satisfaction'. Being now ready for sea, the sailors began to 'deliver their ships themselves', which led to a 'terrible fray' with the coal-heavers. For a period of days 'to so great a height had this insurrection got', that Wapping was under military guard, until nine of the coal-heavers were hanged at Tyburn for murder.

'This example,' remarked Chamberlain in his 18th-century tone, 'produced a happy effect; the tumults immediately ceased, and peace and industry supplied the place of resentment and mischief.'

During the next months, Parliament repeatedly 'rejected Mr. Wilkes, as not being a proper person', and equally repeatedly the Middlesex freemen persisted in re-electing him. Still the House rejected him. And eventually the electors even dared petition the Crown in a remarkable document listing their grievances: arbitrary arrest, misappropriation of public money, the suspension of Habeas Corpus, illegal entry, the fabrication of evidence, imprisonment without trial, military execution, 'mobs and riots hired and raised by the ministry', 'murder abetted, encouraged and rewarded', justice over-ruled by the Crown, 'obsolete and vexatious claims of the Crown set on foot', the establishment of a standing army, and its use in the streets. And in their last paragraph the freemen of Middlesex reached out from their assembly room at Mile-end to touch the wheel of history: 'The same indiscretion has been extended by the same evil counsellors to your majesty's dominions in America, and has produced to our suffering fellow subjects in that part of the world, grievances and apprehensions similar to those of which we complain at home.'

At this time Blake was little over ten, and this was to be the atmosphere of London for a decade or more. So often the mob was controlled (as we saw Wilkes quietly control it in Spitalfields), and self-controlled (as in its dismissal of the tipstaffs), and in control (as in its turning of Wilkes's hackney coach). It was ominous and compelling. The unanswerable justice of the coal-heavers' anger took them inevitably to the end of Tyburn road and the re-establishment of 'peace and industry'. Many were to follow them along the same road, to fulfil the same necessity, almost past Blake's house as he grew to manhood.

In 1760 when George III followed his grandfather as 'the sovereign of a free people' he expressed 'tender concern for the rights, trade and manufactures of the city of London'. And this was all in his capital that the King thought fit to mention as his 'concern'. As Blake grew up in a city always on edge he watched the monarch sidle towards personal power. And gradually not only 'the middling and inferior sort of people' backed John Wilkes, but also the tradesmen and merchants. As the war against his 'majesty's dominions in America' dragged on, the sympathy expressed by the Middlesex freemen at Mile-end turned to open support for the colonies. London was the focal point of revolt against the Court of St. James.

Blake was a republican all his life. He was the child, not of the fashionable salons of his age, but of the turbulent, independent opposition. The war became habitual, and callous hypocrisy a way of life. Soldiers deserted in thousands and the King called in his Hessian mercenaries. During the Gordon riots in the summer of 1780 the mob had London in its fist for days on end. Among others, the crowd broke into the residence of Count Haslang, the Bavarian envoy (who ran a lucrative protection racket on the side), at 23 Golden Square, gaining entrance through the Catholic chapel in the garden at the back of the house. Blake was now twenty-two, and one day in these June riots found himself at the head of the mob that fired Newgate Gaol and released the prisoners. If he was in this affray at all against his wishes, he was certainly not there without sympathy.

The next year Blake went to stay with a market-gardener named Boucher in the 'pleasantly situated' village of Battersea, in open country across the Thames, allegedly to recover from an illness. The move out of London could well have been diplomatic for such a stubborn anti-monarchist. While Blake was 'convalescing', the mayor and aldermen of London declared to the King their 'abhorrence of the continuation of this un-natural and unfortunate war' in America. Blake shared the abhorrence; but whereas the London merchants were concerned for the 'freedom' identified in their charters, Blake's opposition was unqualified and rooted in principle. During this year, how-ever, he was preoccupied with courting the daughter of the Battersea market-gardener and on August 18, 1782, he was married to Catherine Boucher in the newly-rebuilt Battersea church.

3

'Poetical Sketches' (1783)

i

A year after his marriage Blake's first book, *Poetical Sketches*, was printed, but never published, all the sheets being handed to Blake, who disposed of them gradually and privately throughout his life. Twenty-two copies still survive.

Blake's opposition to the political set-up of his day is evident in *King Edward III*, a dramatic dialogue. The King at the outset ironically draws attention to 'Liberty, the chartered right of Englishmen', and expects his 'most righteous cause' to succeed inevitably against an enemy who fought 'in chains, invisible chains, but heavy' because their minds were 'fettered'. In *Songs of Experience* the very phrases concerning charters and intellectual chains are echoed in the devastating condemnation of the situation in London.

In this short imitation of Shakespeare, Blake is already aware of the easy fallacies with which the royal commanders justify their war. They speak with voices recognisably Georgian. In the second scene Clarence describes London and her glories with a sublimity which leaves the reality of degradation and poverty unacknowledged, and which is a parody of contemporary 'poetic' attitudes. He tells how the King, toiling in his wars to guard England's peace,

> . . . turns his eyes on this
> His native shore, and sees Commerce fly round
> With his white wings, and sees his golden London
> And her silver Thames, thronged with shining spires
> And corded ships, her merchants buzzing round

> Like summer bees, and all the golden cities
> In his land overflowing with honey—
> Glory may not be dimmed with clouds of care.
> Say, Lords, should not our thoughts be first to Commerce?
> My Lord Bishop, would you recommend us agriculture?
>
> KING EDWARD III

To this the Bishop has a ready answer:

> When I sit at my home, a private man,
> My thoughts are in my gardens and my fields,
> How to employ the hand that lacketh bread.
> If Industry is in my diocese,
> Religion will flourish.

But letting his 'thoughts take in the general good of the whole', since 'England is the land favoured by Commerce', he recommends 'be England's trade our care'.

A few lines further on Clarence points out how the French

> like to ravening wolves
> Infest our English seas, devouring all
> Our burdened vessels, spoiling our naval flocks.
> The merchants do complain and beg our aid.

Commerce (not liberty or justice) justifies war, and the Bishop justifies commerce, and affirms the divine right of the English as

> sovereigns
> Of the sea—our right that Heaven gave
> To England, when at the birth of nature
> She was seated in the deep, the Ocean ceased
> His mighty roar, and fawning played around
> Her snowy feet and owned his lawful Queen.

In the third scene, at Cressy, the Black Prince praises 'the spirit of liberty' in an Englishman; and Chandos exposes this regal fiction. Liberty means property, social divisions, avarice. All they have to do is to 'teach man to think he's a free agent', and he will 'build himself a hut, and hedge / A spot of ground' and defend it with his blood, 'till glory fires his breast to enlarge his castle'.

30

'Glory' is self-aggrandisement, and 'the spirit of liberty' commercial ambition. At once, however, the King launches into the threadbare battle-cry of all rulers with 'a sacred cause' in every age, catching up inevitably the word 'glory':

> O Liberty, how glorious art thou!
> I see thee hovering o'er my army, with
> Thy wide-stretched plumes.

The satirical echo in Blake's lines could hardly be missed in his day. For decades poets had habitually approved of the stance he gives the established royal commanders. James Thomson in *The Seasons*, one of the most revered long poems of the century, between lines 1440–85 of 'Summer' apostrophises 'happy Britannia' as guardian of Liberty (a land that 'teems with wealth', the 'dread of tyrants'), goes on to name the Edwards, Kings 'dear to fame', as

> the first who deep-impressed
> On haughty Gaul the terror of thy arms—

glances at the naval power of England, and her 'crowded ports', and graces with poetic approval the convenient fictions that trade meant joy for all and labourers built palaces delightedly:

> Full are thy cities with the sons of art;
> And trade and joy in every busy street
> Mingling are heard. Even Drudgery himself
> As at the car he sweats, or dusty hews
> The palace stone, looks gay.

John Dyer had praised the propriety of employing the poor 'in cheerful works of virtuous trade', and described London under its fashionable poetic name, Augusta:

> . . . great Augusta's mart, where lofty trade,
> Amid a thousand golden spires enthroned,
> Gives audience to the world. The strand around
> Close swarms with busy crowds of many a realm.
> What bales, what wealth, what industry, what fleets!
>
> THE FLEECE III, 626–30

31

One comes upon such approved sentiments again and again. Blake had read them till they sickened him; for him the alliance between King George, the bishops, the navy and commercial convenience was tyrannous and its justice as specious as the liberty it claimed to uphold. And from where he looked at them, with the beggar in the street, the 'thousand golden spires' of London could not be seen.

Blake later revived this idealised view of London when he contemplated the city becoming Jerusalem. But whereas the Augusta described by the established poets was a delusive solace concealing a vicious reality, Jerusalem later was a vision, realisable in a change of heart.

ii

It is thought to have been the Reverend A. S. Matthews who prefaced the *Poetical Sketches* with an apology that they were 'the production of untutored youth, commenced in his twelfth and occasionally resumed by the author till his twentieth year'. The minister reported that, although 'conscious of the irregularities and defects to be found in almost every page, his friends have still believed that they possessed a poetic originality, which merited some respite from oblivion'.

The 'irregularities and defects' would be measured inevitably against the accepted standards of elegant taste. Since he could not enjoy our hindsight, Matthews could hardly be expected to recognise the implications of the 'poetic originality' that appears even as early as this.

Blake's uniqueness and strangeness have been for so long stressed that it is important to emphasise how conventional some of the *Poetical Sketches* are. Blake wrote later with such uncompromising originality that the ordinariness of the beginning is often forgotten; forgotten too is the fact that his unique and revolutionary way of thinking is not something he adopted later, but is present in some of these very early poems. *Poetical Sketches* are therefore interesting for apparently contradictory reasons.

They open with four short poems on the seasons. Here Blake is

following a favourite contemporary exercise. Spring is apostro-
phised with a mock holiness that is commonplace in 18th-century
pastoral:

> O thou with dewy locks, who lookest down
> Through the clear windows of the morning, turn
> Thine angel eyes upon our western isle
> Which in full choir hails thy approach, O Spring.

It is all so poetically correct. By contrast, in *Mad Song* Blake
follows the vogue for mock frenzy. It is a reflection of the interest
in atmosphere that was highly charged, expensive and weird.
But it is as artificial as the useless follies built on hill-tops to
provide a pseudo-Gothic decoration to a landscape. The emotion
is unreal:

> Like a fiend in a cloud
> With howling woe,
> After night I do crowd
> And with night will go;
> I turn my back to the east
> From whence comforts have increased,
> For light doth seize my brain
> With frantic pain.

Just as in pastoral verse certain phrases were prescribed—'early
morn walks forth', 'pensive woe', 'silent shade', 'sprightly
dance', so here phrases such as 'howling woe' and 'frantic pain'
anticipated their own appearance. The language inhibited thought
and offered the consolation of a familiar response, a kind of
automatic poetry, comprehensible at sight. Even in *Poetical
Sketches*, Blake recognised the sterility of these poetic good
manners, and had his own comment to make. In *To the Muses* he
delivered the rebuke in lines as mannered as the verse they
condemn. It is as if Blake writes fourteen lines of model versification unexceptionable in contemporary judgment, then, having
shown what it is like, dismisses it in the last two lines.

> Whether on Ida's shady brow,
> Or in the chambers of the east,

The chambers of the sun, that now
From ancient melody have ceased;

Whether in Heaven ye wander fair,
Or the green corners of the earth,
Or the blue regions of the air,
Where the melodious winds have birth;

Whether on crystal rocks ye rove,
Beneath the bosom of the sea,
Wandering in many a coral grove,
Fair Nine, forsaking poetry!

How have you left the ancient love
That bards of old enjoyed in you!
The languid strings do scarcely move!
The sound is forced, the notes are few!

TO THE MUSES

Blake recognised what the poetry of his day had come to—the
expected thought in the appropriate phrase. And already in
Poetical Sketches he begins to resolve the dilemma. In the verses
we have so far looked at, each word is so well-behaved that we
are only aware of its preciosity. Each word has become a sign
indicating a received idea. Language has lost the quality of
surprise, and tension is excluded as the lines repeat themselves
with a deserted sameness of mood. But there is a hint of Blake's
unpleasantly searching directness in the complete reconciliation
of object and action that goes so far beyond the polite personifications of his contemporaries, in *How sweet I roamed from field
to field*. Here the bird, captive, displayed and mocked, is directly
symbolic of possessive love, and has Blake's own essential quality.
At the outset the reader feels uncomfortable. There is a hint of
betrayal from the beginning, once we read that freedom was
sweet *until* the speaker saw the Prince of Love. The second
stanza confirms the suspicion, with its blushing roses, gardens
and golden pleasures of temptation. The transition from a child
speaking, to a bird in a cage, is made without explanation. But it is
completely effective because the conceptual parallel between

the child's state and the bird's is so clear. The identity of the Prince of Love is ambiguous. Not vague, as personification usually is, but ambiguous, because it may mean so many things at once. The child who was tempted by the Prince of Love suddenly becomes the bird. There is no attempt to write in a few lines of transition, and yet we feel no shock of abruptness. Our minds are held by the conceptual significance of the actions related, and not dominated by the physical presence of the speaker, boy or bird. The solicitude of the first two stanzas shifts uncomfortably into the attentiveness of the last two. A link exists at the powerfully felt, intellectual core of the poem. It is the kind of unity we will find time and again in Blake's poems, an uncompromising strength of thought or feeling that controls and limits the physical impact of his symbols, and fuses apparently contradictory or unrelated references into a tense conceptual unity. This is the supreme quality of great poems like *The Sick Rose* and *The Tiger*, and it is fundamental already in one or two *Poetical Sketches:*

> How sweet I roamed from field to field
> And tasted all the summer's pride,
> Till I the Prince of Love beheld
> Who in the sunny beams did glide!
>
> He showed me lilies for my hair,
> And blushing roses for my brow;
> He led me through his gardens fair
> Where all his golden pleasures grow.
>
> With sweet May dews my wings were wet,
> And Phoebus fired my vocal rage,
> He caught me in his silken net,
> And shut me in his golden cage.
>
> He loves to sit and hear me sing;
> Then, laughing, sports and plays with me;
> Then stretches out my golden wing
> And mocks my loss of liberty.

We are likely to say at first of this poem that we do not understand it. What we mean (by comparison with conventional verse

which we understand easily) is that it leads us into areas of surmise that we have not previously explored. Suddenly, we sense
that a poem has the quality of greatness, that it engages speculation
and defies immediate comprehension. The further we go into it,
the further the poem seems to stretch.

If, as B. H. Malkin (who knew Blake) wrote in 1806, the poem
'was written before the age of fourteen' it is even more remarkable and important.

Moreover, Malkin's assertion must put us on our guard against
assuming a biographical significance in a poem. We will say
more of this later on. In the meantime, however, if we did not
have Malkin's statement, it would be almost irresistible to inter-
pret this poem as a comment upon Blake's recent marriage, the
'golden cage' being what he later called 'matrimony's golden
cage'. Indeed, much of the symbolism (the roses, the gardens,
the silken net and the cage) is later associated by Blake with the
alluring yet jealous capitivity within which man can be held by
woman.

However, there is no reason to disbelieve Malkin, and no
reason to think that Blake in 1782 saw his marriage as captivity.
This leads us to a more important initial point: it is that this
symbolism associated with authority (parental or religious),
temptation, illusory promises, and gentle snares in his immature
years, is transferred in his maturity to represent the different (but
no less dangerous) authority and the deceptive assurances that
beset the grown man. It is something quite different from Wordsworth's poetic use of childhood experience.

No matter what incident we may surmise stimulated the poem,
it draws attention to three essential qualities in the poet's way of
thinking, and proves these three qualities to be quite natural to
him.

First, as a boy, before he can have read much poetry or thought
about it seriously, he already uses symbols and identifies a concept with a percept. The effect of some powerful influence
(Christian teaching, paternal command, a divine vision, sexual
awareness) is identified in the actions in the tempting garden,

the trapping of the bird and the mocking admiration. The boy and the bird are both symbolic victims.

Second, even as early as this Blake shows an instinctive tendency to transfer a personal experience into a sequence of symbolic actions by suppressing the circumstance that initiated the poem, in the imaginative act of inducing an uncomfortable recognition on the part of the reader. Again the contrast with Wordsworth, who fixes the reader's attention upon his own experience, rather than transferring that experience to the reader, is complete.

Third, there are already in this poem some startling associations of ideas that anticipate the powerful and disturbing symbolism of the poems of Experience. Fields, open and unfenced, are associated with spiritual freedom and innocence; the rose and gardens with the temptations fostered by possessive love; the net and the golden cage with the deprival of intellectual liberty. And already the poet disdains the explicit slackness of a simile; pleasures do not grow *like* golden flowers.

So Blake was a poet long before he was a philosopher, and he was thinking in symbols long before he was aware of mysticism. Blake did not arrive at a philosophy and then artificially invent a symbolic system for its exposition. The priority is important. The poet precedes the philosopher and mystic, and this single poem seems to me to invalidate all the commentaries that begin in an attempt to elucidate Blake's philosophy and then relate it to the poetry. Blake's philosophy was experience to him, and it was realised in the poetry. And conversely his experience (as here in early youth) was realised in poetry to raise unpleasant philosophical doubts. To attempt to isolate and formulate Blake's philosophy is a barren exercise.

iii

The concentration in the symbolism of the song *Love and harmony combine* and the assurance with which Blake assumes that the reader's imagination will grasp the essential meaning is unprecedented in 18th-century poetry. Already Blake is writing a poem that is not a description, but an experience; the symbolism does not represent a series of abstract ideas. It does not simply describe a relationship, but involves us in a relationship; we acquire a realisation that this is what such-and-such a relationship or experience can be or is.

Moreover, the words are simple. They draw no attention to themselves, and the verse is not sophisticated. The words have to be simple to carry the charge of their meaning; it is the meaning that is challenging. The more we read, the more we comprehend, and our experience seems to extend. This is, of course, true of all great poetry; but Blake's particular quality is the unrelenting immediacy of the imaginative challenge. Relationships, feelings, fears, joys exist in symbols, and action is fundamental. The words 'combine' and 'entwine' lead the imagination towards realisation so subtly and certainly that the branches appear almost as if auto-suggested:

Love and harmony combine
And around our souls entwine,
While thy branches mix with mine
And our roots together join.

Joys upon our branches sit,
Chirping loud and singing sweet;
Like gentle streams beneath our feet
Innocence and virtue meet.

Thou the golden fruit dost bear,
I am clad in flowers fair;
Thy sweet boughs perfume the air,
And the turtle buildeth there.

There she sits and feeds her young,
Sweet I hear her mournful song;
And thy lovely leaves among—
There is love: I hear his tongue.

There his charming nest doth lay,
There he sleeps the night away,
There he sports along the day,
And doth among our branches play.

iv

Some of the songs in *Poetical Sketches* inspired by Blake's courtship and early days of marriage are undistinguished. Songs like
I love the jocund dance and *Fresh from the dewy hill, the merry year*
are no better than ordinary 18th-century verse, though more
subjective and personal than most. But the more clearly the
lines reflect an actual incident, the more ordinary the verse
appears.

It has often been said that Blake's poetry is intensely individual
and that this quality marks the beginning of the Romantic age
in poetry. It seems to me a dangerous, misleading generalisation.
Blake certainly thought for himself and expressed views that
were unconventional and revolutionary. But his writing has a
profound social relevance. And even when the poetry is based
directly and obviously on an intense personal experience, we are
led towards the general implications, never back towards an
egotistical commitment.

18th-century poetry at its urbane best, in Pope for instance,
was incisive and social. It questioned manners and social relationships. When Pope's own feelings are engaged, the tension (as in
Elegy to the Memory of an Unfortunate Lady) between these feelings
and the need to keep within literary decorum makes the lines
deeply moving. We can feel the grief, indignation and anger
straining against the social requirements of the verse—rhyme,
paradox, form—and the emotion is fused into an intellectual
triumph. Moreover, even the sentiment itself is an intellectual
triumph. Pope did not need to suffer a personal grief before he
could write his moving *Elegy*. The grief is itself a creation of his
mind, and is buttressed against the hypocrisy of contemporary
attitudes, which it finally breaks down and exposes.

Blake, of course, could never invent a sentiment. He began

always from an actual and intensely felt emotion, or from the effect of emotion in someone else upon himself. And it is true that Blake has little in common with Pope. But in one vital respect he belongs to the 18th century, and is nearer to Pope than to Keats—in that it is not the personal nature of an emotion that is important in Blake's poetry, but the extent of its social implications.

So Blake could tell how 'love and harmony combine' in the carefree Summer of courtship, and the biographical origins of the poem are of no more consequence to its meaning than the full stop before a sentence begins. Here already the reader is made to experience directly the nature of harmony and love, and to recognise in it a universal inclusiveness. From here, it is a short step to *Songs of Innocence*.

It is essentially the same way of thought later, when Blake's poetry moves away from a profoundly felt personal experience (which may be a reaction to social evil) to a fiercely concentrated assault on the falsehoods that inhabit the soul and therefore corrupt society. It is through this that the appalling relevance of Blake's poetry still persists—because the cant it attacks is still rooted. By identifying emotion (jealousy, hatred, greed, cruelty) in symbolism, this poetry simultaneously makes us recognise ourselves in the emotion, and aware of the presence of evil. The poetry leads us, not to the poet's emotion but to the peril of the emotion. The poetry is in the peril. In this Blake is nearer to his predecessors of the 18th, and even 17th, century than he is to Wordsworth or Keats, and seemingly nearer to us.

In *Poetical Sketches*, among much that is ordinary, Blake ironically lets the principles which his age revered (the God of thunder, the ocean ruled by Britannia, the monarchy, the charters of London, episcopacy) speak their own condemnation. And his poetry is already moving in an unprecedented direction.

4

Blake's Poetic Symbolism

i

When we come to read Blake's poetry we must jettison our most cherished assumptions. Most revolutionary writers express their opposition to certain accepted institutions or social codes, and make their opposition clear by justifying their position. They appeal, either to the emotions or the intellect, with an argument that begins with conventional assumptions and then goes on to demonstrate the inadequacy or falsehood of those assumptions. Moreover, they begin from an acceptance of the ordinary received associations that have grown around the language of their day. As we saw in the Introduction, these associations are extremely powerful and dictate the reader's reactions in thought and mood.

Now Blake saw the manacles that bind mankind as 'mind-forged', and among these 'mind-forged manacles' are the dominant sequences of word, thought and reaction that shackle the intellect and imagination, and govern behaviour. Blake began by breaking the shackles of language. Even today some writers maintain that he strained the ordinary meaning of words too far, and that the demands he makes upon the reader are unjustifiable.

While it is impossible to explain what Blake is saying, and pointless to try, it is fairly easy to give the reader the clue to understanding Blake. It is fundamentally no more than a matter of getting rid of preconceptions; Blake might call it 'cleansing the doors of perception'.

First it is essential to distinguish between mythology and

symbolism. By the symbolism I do not mean those immortals with strange names—Enitharmon, Oothoon, Rintrah—who move through Blake's longer poems, mingling with contemporary forgotten men like Hyde and Schofield, and the famous like Washington and Pitt. This invented mythology puzzled the commentators for generations. Fortunately it need not worry us much. Blake used these strangely named figures to represent abstract ideas because he wished at times to avoid the associations of traditional mythology; or he wished to consider an ancient principle from an unprecedented point of view.

This is most readily apparent in the major mythological figure, Urizen, to whom we shall have to refer fairly frequently, as the name summarises the basic philosophy with which Blake identified the evils of his day. Urizen is a sort of Almighty incarnate in George III. Urizen is the tyrannical, sullen, avenging deity, the promulgator of the law of stone, the law of 'thou shalt not'.

Sitting 'beneath the Tree of Mystery in darkest night', Urizen cries to his warriors:

> The Universal ornament is mine, and in my hands
> The ends of heaven; like a garment will I fold them round me,
> Consuming what must be consumed. Then in power and majesty
> I will walk forth through those wide fields of endless Eternity,
> A God and not a Man, a Conqueror in triumphant glory,
> And all the Sons of Everlasting shall bow down at my feet.

In the next line Blake goes on to give the creative acts of this deity, whose majesty and power demands such obedience:

> First Trades and Commerce, ships and armed vessels he builded laborious
> To swim the deep. And on the land, children are sold to trades
> Of dire necessity, still labouring day and night till all
> Their life extinct they took the spectre form in dark despair,
> And slaves in myriads, in shiploads, burden the hoarse sounding deep,
> Rattling with clanking chains.

Urizen orders 'all his myriads' to build 'a temple in the image of the human heart':

> And in the inner part of the Temple, wondrous workmanship,
> They formed the secret place, reversing all the order of delight,
> That whosoever entered into the Temple might not behold
> The hidden wonders, allegoric of the Generations
> Of secret lust, when hid in chambers dark the nightly harlot
> Plays in disguise, in whispered hymn and mumbling prayer. The priests
> He ordained, and priestesses, clothed in disguises bestial
> Inspiring secrecy.

They drag the sun itself into the temple of Urizen:

> To light the war by day, to hide his secret beams by night,
> For he divided day and night, in different ordered portions,
> The day for war, the night for secret religion in his temple.

THE FOUR ZOAS VII, b

In this exposition we are shown many of the major attributes of Urizen. Clearly, few of Blake's contemporaries will acknowledge this god as the deity they worship in their churches. And Blake's problem of communication is seen to be the more difficult when we hear contemporary writers, time and again and quite unquestioningly, extolling the virtues of commerce, its link with Crown and Church, and even recognising the Christian God in trade:

> And when the priest displays, in just discourse
> Him, the all-wise Creator, and declares
> His presence, power and goodness unconfined,
> 'Tis Trade, attentive voyager, who fills
> His lips with argument. To censure Trade,
> Or hold her busy people in contempt,
> Let none presume.

John Dyer, THE FLEECE II, 614–20

It is the merchants, Dyer goes on to say, who 'the clearest sense of Deity receive'. One can say either that this is Urizen regarded with awe and reverence, or that Blake's Urizen is such

43

18th-century gospel seen from a different angle. In the name of the Almighty, or of Urizen, charity was preached in the churches, not out of love, but to establish the poor in a 'useful station of independent poverty', because their services were 'essential in the highest degree to the comfort and convenience of the higher orders of society'. There was economy in charity, as this, the age of organised charities, most clearly saw.

We can see the economy exemplified in The Foundling Hospital, the most imposing memorial of all to 18th-century benevolence. It covered a site of fifty-six acres in Lamb's Conduit Fields, and was completed a few years before Blake was born. Philanthropy was the offspring of a commercial and military necessity. There was concern to maintain a flourishing supply of labour, and any decline in population was considered with horror. The death-rate among children in workhouses exceeded one in two, and The Foundling Hospital achieved a rate of about one in three. The dead children were buried in the spacious cemetery at the back of the hospital, and those who lived were surrounded with paintings glorifying the State, taught a pious obedience, and prepared for labour within 'the bounds of their condition', 'upon which the happiness of the lower orders, no less than that of those in more elevated station, depends'.

It must not be thought that this was heartless. It was not. Those words were written by Patrick Colquhoun, a great social reformer, fifty years later. From 1756–60 The Foundling Hospital chaotic-ally made unlimited admissions in return for a grant from a government concerned about losses in the war with France. And the supply of foundlings to this and other institutions (like the Greycoat Hospital in St. Margaret's, Westminster, to provide 'apprentices to sea-captains in the King's service') was limitless, from the offspring of some 150,000 beggars and 'the pagan inhabitants in the centre of London'.

Presiding over 'the careful State severely Kind' was a monarch addressed in words perhaps more applicable to the Deity. It was George III not God who was addressed 'with reverential awe and gratitude' on June 17, 1761, as 'the supreme giver of all victory', when 'the conquest of Bellisle' seemed to have assured 'the wealth, reputation and independence of this commercial nation'. Blake saw London around him with its clergymen and doctors preaching a morality and economic charity convenient to the comfortable, where Satan, 'being called God', compelled men 'to serve him in moral gratitude and submission', and he was alone in his revulsion. 'The Satanic Holiness', Satan 'being called God', is Urizen. This is the God Blake heard men worshipping in the 'dark Satanic mills'—the churches of his day that were 'mills of Satan', where men 'in his synagogues worship Satan under the unutterable name'. He summarised 'the looms and mills and prisons and workhouses' as 'those churches'.

For Blake's contemporaries, charitable and philanthropic organisations were wholly admirable, and reassuring in the way they were used to confirm and strengthen the established social structure.

Blake saw children kept alive as far as possible in charitable institutions and then 'sold to trade', and declared it evil. But the maintenance of a high population was to most men a fundamental principle of prosperity. Charity and expedience went hand in hand:

> But chief by numbers of industrious hands
> A nation's wealth is counted: numbers raise
> Warm emulation: where that virtue dwells,
> There will be traffic's seat; there will she build
> Her rich emporium.
>
> THE FLEECE III, 530–4

Though self-interest and social preservation lay behind much of the work, many philanthropists were sincere and honestly Christian in their endeavours, within the limits of contemporary assumptions. It is easy for us from a distance of two hundred years to recognise and condemn 'the rooted depravity of a pretended civilisation and a spurious and mock Christianity' that perpetuated the division of man against man and even justified the existence of appalling poverty as divinely ordained. It was

45

even possible for men like Captain J. G. Stedman (whose book on his expedition to South America Blake illustrated and who wrote the words just quoted) to recognise hypocrisy; but even men like Stedman stopped short of the ultimate condemnation.

Only Blake was a 'man without a mask'. For Blake, the god worshipped in the churches was false and his law a device extracted from true Christian teaching. Blake's dilemma is apparent. The morality in question could not be attributed to God or Christ; on the other hand, it could not be attributed to Satan, which would mean judging it against accepted standards of good and evil. He had to give a name to the deity behind the whole moral, philosophical, theological justification of the set-up; and the name he chose was Urizen, the 'God of all this dreadful ruin'.

The identities of Urizen and all the other mythological figures may change from book to book. This seems confusing, but need not be when we appreciate that these figures in two different books represent an idea or principle in different stages of development or decay, or considered by Blake from a different viewpoint. And there is rarely much difficulty (at least for the major figures) in finding out what Blake wants us to understand by a mythological figure because the meaning is substantiated in the poetic symbolism.

ii

We have already seen how extensively a reader's memory will augment or define the meaning of any word or group of words. We have seen that by its very nature symbolism must be familiarly recognisable; a certain percept must be associated quite instinctively by the reader with a certain concept—or at least some aspect of that concept. So the percept *fox* inevitably raises the concept of *cunning*; the percept *lion* equally inevitably raises the concept of *royalty* or *pride*. Already the word 'or' has come in —'or pride'. Already, that is, the normal tendency of linguistic associations to slip their definitions, to refuse to be confined, is taking effect. This seems at first glance to make things difficult,

46

as it is clearly going to be impossible to label each symbol with a precise meaning. In fact, it is precisely this quality that makes *poetic* symbolism possible. A symbol is not reduced to an emblem.

'Salt as incorruptible,' wrote Sir Thomas Browne in the 17th century, conveniently for us explaining as he went along—'Salt as incorruptible was the symbol of friendship.' So we see that a certain aspect or quality of the percept *salt* makes it a symbol in which a certain quality of friendship is realised. At once the reader sees the relevance; and it is not so much that the reader consciously excludes other qualities of salt (its solubility, its taste, its preservative powers) as that these qualities do not enter the mind. The imagination is focused on the immediate relevance.

We notice, moreover, that Sir Thomas Browne's symbol also conveys his attitude (for the time being anyway) to friendship. We understand that he sees it as incorruptible. We also see that he has to explain this quite clearly, in case salt may not be familiar to us as a symbol relating to incorruptibility.

Now if a writer uses the symbol *fox* for cunning we instinctively exclude all other irrelevant aspects of the fox, because we are familiar with this association of ideas. Moreover, we accept that the writer is usually disapproving, and there would be little need to explain it, as the percept, and the concept, and the attitude of mind expressed in the usage are well established in our common awareness. Similarly in the 18th century if a writer mentioned *thunder* in connection with the wrath of God, it is clear that he would do so in obedient acceptance of divine justice. If he did not accept the justice of God's thunder, he would have to explain this, and in doing so would lose the immediacy and focus of the symbolism.

Here, precisely, is Blake's dilemma and the challenge of his poetry. For Blake *thunder* is a symbol of divine wrath; but the god of thunder is Urizen, and Blake does not grant that his thunder is just. Yet he cannot wait to reason; he is not concerned with propositions and arguments, but with relationships and effects. As he said himself: 'I will not reason and compare: my business is to create.' And 'to create' he needs the symbolism to be immediate in its impact, and above all he needs the reader to apprehend his meaning by an imaginative response, to recreate the indignation, sense of tragedy, the desolation in the mind of the man who wrote the words. An intellectual prettiness, a clever notion is not enough.

So if Blake used established symbols he was bound to 'unsay' the established attitude of mind to these symbols. Alternatively he had to create a symbolism of his own, by establishing fresh associations. And since it is essential that a symbol be instinctively recognised, he could only do this by repetition.

iii

The points I have been labouring are made clear if we turn to one or two examples of Blake's symbolism. Again it must be stressed that we should not seek to define a symbol precisely, and apply that definition wherever it occurs. The meaning of a symbol is turned into a different focus as the poet's attack shifts its ground. Qualifying phrases or situations lead us from primary to secondary meanings. There is truth and false truth. All around him Blake saw

> A pretence of Art to destroy Art; a pretence of Liberty
> To destroy Liberty; a pretence of Religion to destroy Religion.
>
> JERUSALEM II, 43

The difficulty was that few men were aware of the pretence, and fewer still had expressed their awareness. And the pretence had become settled as truth in a long and established practice among poets.

We have already noticed (page 14) how the meaning of the sunrise was qualified as Experience developed. The same thing happens time and again with Blake's symbolism. No catalogue of symbols will do anything but falsify and belittle the poetry, and it is only misleading to yield, as have many scholars, to the temptation to find simple rules of guidance. So in 1928 Joseph Wicksteed explained how 'this life is ever symbolised by the vegetable creation—the grass, the flowers, the rushes and above all by the trees and forests, because it grows up from water and earth and its life is confined to the blind increase of growth and reproduction'. (*Blake's Innocence and Experience*, page 37.) But this theory of a 'fairly simple symbolic method' is disproved by the poetry itself—even by the simple exercise of relating Wicksteed's assertion to the poem *Love and harmony combine* on page 38. Wicksteed asserts that 'the things that to common understanding seem solid and substantial like the material world Blake symbolises as water, dew, mist. For the material world is in perpetual flux. The things that appear abstract like Reason he symbolises as stone, and finally as mountains (imaginative things are sometimes marble) because of their unyielding character' (pp. 70–71). But Blake wrote of 'cold floods of abstraction', 'clouds of reason', 'each strong limb bound down as with marble', and 'coldness, darkness, obstruction . . . black as marble of Egypt'. The rule does not work.

The symbolism will not be defined like this. By defining poetic symbolism we deny the writer that very associative quality of language upon which his work depends. Indeed, the greater the poetry, the further it seems to radiate in the reader's imagination.

The best way, indeed the only way, to apprehend what Blake says, is to read the poetry itself, preferably in an order roughly chronological, since the symbolism and the philosophy (if that is the right word) develop simultaneously. But with this *caveat* in mind we might look briefly at one or two of Blake's more common symbols.

iv

field, hill, valley, meadow, plain, green
Such words form the landscape of Innocence, and are readily comprehensible. They still call to our minds uninhibited joy and freedom, as they could do in Blake's day. In *Poetical Sketches* the line 'How sweet I roamed from field to field' speaks

unrestrained delight that is later lost in captivity, however carefully tended. In *Songs of Innocence* the landscape is predominantly field, valley and hill, in poems like *The Echoing Green, Nurse's Song*, and *The Lamb*. In *The Chimney Sweeper* when the sweep-boys are set free they run 'down a green plain leaping'. In *Laughing Song* the uninhibited delight of childhood in Innocence is transmitted quite naturally to the surrounding landscape, and 'the meadows laugh with lively green'.

In *A Song of Liberty* Blake has the line:

Albion's coast is sick silent; the American meadows faint!

For Blake, a life-long Republican, America signified freedom, and, following the War of Independence, opposition to tyranny. We shall see how cliffs, caverns, shores, rocks and coast, in association with the sea are part of the symbolism of material and spiritual oppression. Sickness and silence indicate the influence of Urizen, which here not only dominates monarchist England, but afflicts the American meadows of freedom and Innocence.

In *Tiriel*, written about the same time as *Songs of Innocence*, Myratana, the wife of Tiriel, a minor deity representing the superstitions of religion, is 'fading in death', who was 'once the queen of all the western plains'. In *The Four Zoas*, dated 1797, Urizen surveys the 'poor ruined world'

Where Joy sang in the trees and pleasure sported in the rivers,
And Laughter sat beneath the oaks, and Innocence sported round
Upon the green plains.

This symbolism is clearly straightforward.

garden, rose

The garden is a symbol providing the location of Love in Experience. Even in *How sweet I roamed from field to field* already the garden is a temptation leading to captivity, and the flower of experienced love, the 'blushing rose', is growing there. In *Tiriel* Har and Heva (the two daughters) sit in 'the pleasant gardens of Har' 'like two children':

> Playing with flowers and running after birds they spent the day,
> And in the night like infants slept, delighted with infant dreams.

The false innocence in the garden is apparent.

The garden is constantly recalled in *Songs of Experience*. In the garden, mankind is walled or fenced off from his neighbour; he tends his own desires, particularly self-conscious affections and jealousies. The garden is a sickly consolation among the evils of London; there are 'soft gardens', 'secret gardens'; in a 'garden of delight' mankind is surrounded by shadows. Urizen himself 'planted a garden of fruits'. This is Eden, never associated with Innocence, but always with temptation, the tree of mystery and forbidden knowledge. This aspect of Eden is the prototype of Blake's symbol of the garden.

The rose is essentially the floral symbol of experienced love. It does not occur at all in *Songs of Innocence*, and as far as I know, Blake never writes of the *wild* rose. It represents love in the gardens of Urizen, fostered and tended with a sense of guilt and shame, protected from other men, open to intrusion. The symbol is most powerfully used in *Songs of Experience*, where Blake explores many aspects of the symbol with disturbing effect, especially in *The Sick Rose*, *My Pretty Rose-tree*, *The Lily* and *The Garden of Love*.

In literature the rose has for centuries been a symbol of love. Proverbially too we have 'No rose without a thorn', and 'The fairest rose is withered'. But in Blake's poetry the conceptual meaning of the flower intensifies as it is related to other symbols. It is not accidental that the rose of Experience grows behind walls in gardens blighted by the winds of pestilence, and is jealously and secretly nursed, because the division of mankind into cities, his suspicious fear of his neighbour, breeding animosity, and his self-interested, inbred affections are consequences symbolic and actual of Urizen's tyranny. The symbolism is organically related; that is, one symbol sustains and strengthens another.

In the symbols of the garden and the rose we see this happening. It is the only way Blake could successfully take two familiar symbols, with the most powerful associations already established in the reader's mind, and so turn our habitual vision, that we sense the appalling hypocrisy of our delicate preconceptions unfurling in our imagination.

forest, tree, myrtle

The forest that came to overgrow the hills of Innocence with its impenetrable superstition is one of Blake's most powerful symbols. The conventional beginning is seen in *Poetical Sketches*, where the 'thickest shades' provide concealment from the sun in *To Summer*, and in *To the Evening Star* the lion 'glares through the dun forest'. This poem is typical in its refined holiness of one 18th-century mannerism Blake soon outgrew. In *Songs of Innocence* the groves (not quite forests) of *Night* and *The Little Black Boy* still occur in a religious context, and we are moving towards the mention in *America* (1793) where the Royalist oppressors crouch terrified in their caverns because

> They cannot smite the wheat, nor quench the fatness of the earth;
> They cannot smite with sorrows, nor subdue the plow and spade;
> They cannot wall the city, nor moat round the castle of princes;
> They cannot bring the stubbed oak to overgrow the hills,

being faced as they are with the 'terrible men', Washington, Paine and Warren.

In those few lines we see how integrated the symbolism is. Caves and caverns often provide shelter for creatures subservient to Urizen: blight, famine, grief, barrenness, walls of exclusion and fortifications all derive from him. In the last line the hills of Innocence are threatened with 'the secret forests', as they were called in *Tiriel*.

In *Visions of the Daughters of Albion* (1793) the questions are asked:

> With what sense does the parson claim the labour of the farmer?
> What are his nets and gins and traps; and how does he surround him
> With cold floods of abstraction and with forests of solitude
> To build him castles and high spires, where Kings and priests may
> dwell?

52

In *Europe* (1794) 'all-devouring fiery Kings' roam 'in dark and desolate mountains, In forests of eternal death', and when mankind sees the serpent in his own desires he conceals himself 'in forests of the night'. In *The Book of Ahania* (1795) we watch these 'forests of affliction' grow from one 'root of mystery' under Urizen's heel, and spread until

> He beheld himself compassed round
> And high roofed over with trees,

and this 'accursed Tree of Mystery' still flourished,

> Enrooting itself all around,
> An endless labyrinth of woe.

This shows the philosophical origin of the forest symbol; but Blake's symbolism was invariably related to social and physical reality. So radical thinkers in Blake's day were objecting to the continuing existence of vast royal forests and heavily-wooded estates, which spread over hills and valleys and which could well have been cleared and the land given to farmers.

In perhaps the most famous of all Blake's poems, the tiger of uninhibited spiritual revolt arises among 'the eternal forests' of Urizen, the Satanic Holiness:

> Tiger! Tiger! burning bright
> In the forests of the night.

Blake's use of the single tree as a symbol demonstrates how impossible it is to define the meaning of each percept. Yet it is never incomprehensible. The meaning of the tree in *Love and harmony combine* in *Poetical Sketches* could not be further from Urizen's 'Tree of Mystery'. Yet the change presents no difficulty. The joy implicit in the symbol in the early poems, in *Fair Elenor* or *The Blossom*, is vitiated in Experience. As the idea of the Tree of Mystery cultivated in the garden occupies Blake's imagination, we can see the symbol qualified through such poems as *The Human Abstract*, *A Poison Tree*, *I feared the fury of my mind*, *Infant Sorrow*, *In a Myrtle Shade* and *To my Myrtle*. And then in *The*

Four Zoas we have the pathetic glance back across the intervening years, to the days when once 'Joy sang on the trees'.

pestilence, net, loom, web

John Armstrong, M.D., a friend of Henry Fuseli the eccentric friend of Blake (he found Blake's ideas 'damned good to steal from'), published a poem in 1744 on *The Art of Preserving Health*. In the first thirty-five lines he links caves (the 'chambers of the globe'), the sea, the forest, avenging heaven, secrecy, comets and the influence of the stars, and names them all as breeding pestilence. It is an unexciting trite progression of ideas, and is the dull, commonplace, 18th-century thinking that leads to Blake's symbolism. Even the phrases 'shapes of death' and the slowly beating wings approach the idea of Urizen:

> Whatever shapes of death,
> Shook from the hideous chambers of the globe,
> Swarm through the shuddering air; whatever plagues
> Or meagre famine breeds, or with slow wings
> Rise from the putrid watery element,
> The damp waste forest, motionless and rank,
> That smothers earth and all the breathless winds,

—these all fly the 'pure effulgence' of Hygeia (Goddess of Health), these and 'all the secret poisons of avenging heaven', despite 'the comet's glare' and 'planets ill-combined'.

The 18th century saw disease and poverty as inevitable; men ascribed sickness to God's retribution and submitted. Blake saw the misery as the outcome of man's inhumanity, and denounced Urizen, the god of vengeance, as a tyrannous deity who grew out of the human brain.

In *Poetical Sketches* Blake is already telling in *Gwin, King of Norway* how

> The nobles of the land did feed
>   Upon the hungry poor;
> They tear the poor man's lamb and drive
>   The needy from their door.

The poem contains much incipient symbolism, and

> Gwin leads his host, as black as night,
>   When pestilence does fly.

This association of the invisible pestilence bred in the dark with the spiritual effects of false religion is the basis of that frightening short poem *The Sick Rose*. In *Europe*, Enitharmon, the woman ruling man by sexual blackmail, calls up her 'luring bird of Eden . . . silent love . . . sweet smiling pestilence . . . sweet perfumes . . . silken queen'.

So Blake, in his disturbing way, uses the symbol to relate religious and sexual tyranny. And this unhealthy erotic implication is also present in *The Sick Rose*, adding yet another level of meaning to those fearsome few lines.

In *The Book of Urizen* the inhabitants of the cities the god has created are afflicted by 'swift diseases' beneath his 'dark net of infection'. The net is another symbol of Urizen's subtle danger; this, too, becomes associated with the shadowy female, Urizen's confederate, who spreads 'nets in every secret path'. The 'silken net' in *How sweet I roamed from field to field* already suggests the trap of tenderness.

The repetition of this very phrase in *Visions of the Daughters of Albion* indicates how misleading it may be to isolate the symbols as we are doing now. There Oothoon (who represents woman's instinctive love) promises to spread 'silken nets and traps of adamant' to catch for her lover 'girls of mild silver or of furious gold'. It seems odd, till we turn to the context which shows Oothoon refuting the corrosive sin of jealousy.

More clearly in the same poem we meet the parson's 'nets and gins and traps', and are told how the 'child of night and sleep', taught 'subtle modesty', comes forth

>   . . . a modest virgin, knowing to dissemble,
>   With nets found under thy night pillow, to catch virgin joy
>   And brand it with the name of whore, and sell it in the night,
>   In silence, even without a whisper, and in seeming sleep.
>   Religious dreams and holy vespers light thy smoky fires.

The 18th century sought in public works to salve its conscience

over prostitution, poverty and disease. For Blake it was hypocrisy, while the old order perpetuated itself, and an oppressive
social and moral code fostered the destitution and traffic in childhood that all professed to deplore:

> These were the Churches, Hospitals, Castles, Palaces,
> Like nets and gins and traps to catch the joys of Eternity,
>   And all the rest a desert,
> Till, like a dream, Eternity was obliterated and erased.
>
> THE SONG OF LOS, AFRICA

Illusions and dreams were consolations encouraged under
Urizen's 'net of religion', 'the dark net of infection'. The latent
association between the dream, darkness, religion and the action
of weaving occurs in a Song of Innocence, *A Dream:*

> Once a dream did weave a shade
> O'er my angel-guarded bed.

In *Milton* (*c.* 1804) Enitharmon's 'looms vibrate with soft
affections, weaving the web of life'. In *Jerusalem* (1804–20) Albion
hypocritically declares that 'all is eternal death unless you can
weave a chaste Body over an unchaste mind',

> That the deep wound of sin might be closed up with the needle
> And with the loom.

In *The Four Zoas* Enion 'thought to weave a covering for my
sins', and

> Urizen heard the voice and saw the shadow underneath
> His woven darkness. And in laws and deceitful religions,
> Beginning at the tree of Mystery, circling its root
> She spread herself through all the branches . . .

and 'the direful web of religion', steeped 'in tears of sorrow
ncessant', fell from heaven upon mankind, until

>   . . . hungry desire and lust began
> Gathering the fruit of that mysterious tree, till Urizen
> Sitting within his temple, furious, felt the numbing stupor,
> Himself tangled in his own net, in sorrow, lust, repentance.
>
> THE FOUR ZOAS VIII

The symbols run together. The loom, with the action of weaving, the web and the net represent the soft delusive terror of sexual dominance. Its sequel is mortification and sorrow, and is identified at times in the vague web of Urizen's false and mysterious moral code, generating its own sins beneath a curtain of erotic righteousness. If this puzzles the reader, he takes the wrong Sunday papers.

stars, mill

In Blake's poetry the stars are never romantic. At one level, as we have seen, the stars and darkness were commonly assumed to endanger health, and Blake related this threat to the malign influence of false doctrines. In *Gwin, King of Norway*, the King's men are 'like blazing comets scattering death Through the red feverous night', and in *Europe* 'the overflowing stars rain down prolific pains'.

However, the symbol soon takes on another dimension, being associated with material repression, then spiritual oppression. The idea arises from the notion of the infinite being mathematically and materially ordered along fixed paths and in calculable and numbered stations. This reflects Blake's reaction to Newtonian physics and the mechanistic universe, as well as to the Bible.

An occasional name Blake gave to Urizen was Newton's Pantocrator (Almighty Power). It was of course accepted unquestioningly that God was ruler of earth and skies, and that he established and ordered the universe. The act of dividing, measuring, directing was for Blake essentially an act of oppression, contrary to the infinite aspirations of imagination. It was Urizen at work.

In 1709 that prolific versifier and nonconformist minister, the 'pious, learned and ingenious' Dr. Isaac Watts (whose hymns we still sing), addressed God as

Lord of the armies of the sky
  He marshals all the stars.
Red comets lift their banners high
  And wide proclaim his wars.

So Blake did not invent the association of the stars with war and material force. He simply usurped a convention. In *The French Revolution* the Royalist power is 'this great starry harvest of six thousand years', the Royal army 'the starry hosts'. In the same poem we have 'each star appointed for watchers of night'. In *A Song of Liberty* 'the starry king' 'leading his starry hosts through the waste wilderness' is a sort of Urizen, crowned George III.

In *The Four Zoas* III, Urizen is asked

> Why sighs my lord? Are not the morning stars thy obedient sons?
> Do they not bow their bright heads at thy voice? At thy command
> Do they not fly into their stations?

In Night V of the same poem, Urizen laments:

> I hid myself in black clouds of my wrath,
> I called the stars around my feet in the night of councils dark;
> The stars threw down their spears and fled naked away.

In the light of this (and especially after what Dr. Watts wrote) all the controversy on the meaning of the famous fifth verse of *The Tiger* becomes irrelevant.

In Urizen's universe the stars, 'numbered all According to their various powers', travelled 'in silent majesty along their ordered ways'. The god delegates his powers at times to Enitharmon, 'the nameless shadowy female', who can sing:

> The joy of woman is the death of her most best beloved
> Who dies for love of her
> In torments of fierce jealousy and pangs of adoration.
> The lovers' night bears on my song
> And the nine spheres rejoice beneath my powerful control.
>
> THE FOUR ZOAS II

Enitharmon, armed with the authority of Urizen, dominates through the night 'in rapturous delusive trance'. At the same time, Oothoon, who delights in freedom is 'bound In spells of law to

58

one she loathes' and is compelled 'all the night To turn the wheel of false desire'.

The symbols of star and wheel combine, based upon the ancient metaphor of the revolving year, the seasons. Man and woman sit in discontent, 'Craving the more, the more enjoying, drawing out sweet bliss From all the turning wheels of heaven'.

Man shrinks away from 'the wheels of turning darkness'. And the 'Prince of the Starry Wheels'—

Prince of the Starry hosts
And of the wheels of heaven, to turn the mills day and night,
MILTON I, 4

is Satan (here called Newton's Pantocrator), whose work is 'eternal death with mills and ovens and cauldrons', and who has 'a scheme of human conduct invisible and incomprehensible' for mortals, to whom his mills 'seem everything'. Satan at this stage is close to Urizen, and these quotations are only a page or so away from the famous lines beginning 'And did those feet in ancient time'. The 'dark Satanic mills' are these mills, and the 'miller of Eternity' is Satan-as-Urizen.

We have seen the relationship between the stars, pestilence, war, oppression, false desire, the cosmic wheel, the harsh law of Urizen, and the eternal mills of Satan. The symbolism works both at infinite range and with intimate effect. The abstract doctrine is given immediate relevance. And the 'mills of Satan' are not only the places where 'the sun and moon receive their fixed destinations' but also predestine mankind to obedient servitude along the Thames among Albion's temples,

Where Satan, making to himself laws from his own identity,
Compelled others to serve him in moral gratitude and submission,
Being called God, setting himself above all that is called God;
And all the spectres of the dead, calling themselves sons of God,
In his synagogues worship Satan under the Unutterable Name.
MILTON I, 12

In the century before Blake's, von Logau, a German poet, had written

Gottesmühlen mahlen langsam, mahlen aber trefflich klein

—God's mills grind slowly, but they grind exceeding fine.
   Once again, it is not that Blake invented a symbol; he simply
saw behind an old truism a truth that no one dared to face. It is
this that makes him both a visionary and a poet.

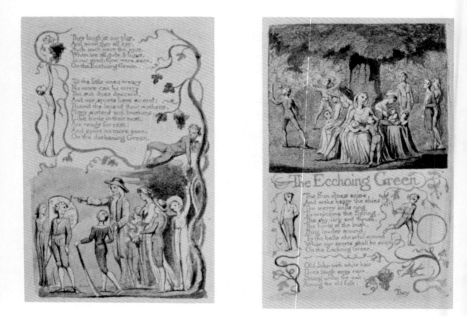

A poem probably inspired by Wimbledon Common from *Songs of Innocence*, 1789,
which was the first book Blake issued through his own method of 'Illuminated
Printing'—   relief etching on copper followed by tinting and water-colour

5

Satire and Innocence

i

In 1784 Blake set up in partnership with James Parker, and with the untrained but willing help of Catherine opened a print shop at 27 Broad Street next door to his old home. The money for the venture came from a legacy Blake had on his father's death in July, and his younger brother, Robert, to whom he was devoted, shared in the venture as a pupil.

During the next two or three years Blake came closer to material success than at any time in his life. There was money in the business and the firm was prepared to supply the fashionable, decorously-erotic prints of Venus, Zephyr and Flora. But by 1787 the venture was finished, Robert was dead and Blake had moved to 28 Poland Street.

However, the optimism of 1784, if harsh and overstrung, is reflected in the satirical *An Island in the Moon*, which Blake wrote at the end of the year. It was a year of promise and optimism nationally, as well as personally for Blake.

If we cannot identify all the characters in *An Island in the Moon* with certainty, we know some; and the prototypes (if not the identities) of others are not far to seek. In this satire Blake is ridiculing the absurdities and hypocrisies of the learned, artistic, scientific sets of his day. As Quid the Cynic, he includes himself in the satire.

For a while Blake has turned away from the oppression and injustice that surrounds him, to regard his friends and the acquaintances among whom they moved. We can savour the satire if we know something of the people it attacks. Yet the atmosphere is strained and constricting. The ridicule is hectic and violently clever; but the satire is neither totally destructive, because it destroys only in the caricatures it inflates, nor creative in its effect, because it lacks magnanimity. Here the work differs in kind from Blake's great poetry. *An Island in the Moon* is uncomfortably odd, provoking but not disturbing; we are confined in the satire, not faced with the revelation of unfathomable evil. The satire talks in its times; the poetry speaks out of them.

When we relate the poetry to contemporary thought and events, we are aware of an evil that persists; there is a real, not simply a tenuous, continuity across the centuries to our own day. When we look at the ephemeral manners and preoccupations that are the target of Blake's satire, we are fascinated by them, trapped into 1784. There is nothing of the timeless relevance that the poetry gives to history. Yet some of the poems in *Songs of Innocence* were written originally for *An Island in the Moon*, and this should rouse our initial curiosity, as on the face of it these two books could hardly be more different.

Perhaps the most remarkable building in Blake's London, certainly the most startling, was the Pantheon, opened in 1772 in Oxford Street, with a side entrance in Poland Street. A vast building, with a glazed dome like the Pantheon of Rome, Ionic and Corinthian columns, ceilings and panels 'painted like Raphael's *loggias* in the Vatican', 'stuccos in the best taste of grotesque, assembly rooms, galleries and statues framed in tabernacles', it 'engrossed the conversation of the polite world' while the American War was fought to a collapse. At first 'the recommendation of a Peeress' was needed for admission, but this had to be dropped 'on account of the rigour with which ladies of easy virtue were exempted from admission'. The come-down across the decade in attendance at the Pantheon from ambassadors and the Lord Chancellor to 'a very numerous assembly of fashionable people' was sad, but human and inevitable.

The mood of the times in 1783 was exemplified in the 'elegant structure' placed in the Great Room 'dedicated to Peace', and 'chiefly composed of warlike implements, now rendered useless'.

On September 15, 1784, Vincenzo Lunardi, the 'first aerial traveller in the English atmosphere', rose in his balloon from the Artillery Ground in Moorfields, floated over London 'about the size of a tennis ball', and came down at Ware. He was lifted by hydrogen (then called 'inflammable air, or gas') supplied by Dr. George Fordyce, chemist and physician at St. Thomas's Hospital, who lived on one magnificent meal a day, and often operated all morning after celebrating all night. When Blake was writing *An Island in the Moon* Lunardi's balloon was on show in the Pantheon, and 'balloon hats', which the Islander Miss Gittipin so envied, were all the rage. And Inflammable Gass the Windfinder, another Islander, was busy, like Joseph Priestley (or George Fordyce), 'with glasses and brass tubes and magic pictures'.

Familiar to the Islanders too was Jack Tearguts—'he understands anatomy better than any of the ancients', Blake wrote. 'He'll plunge his knife up to the hilt in a single drive and thrust his fist in, and all in the space of a quarter of an hour. He does not mind their crying—though they cry ever so he'll swear at them and keep them down with his fist and tell them that he'll scrape their bones if they don't lay still and be quiet. What the devil should the people in the hospital that have it done for nothing make such a piece of work for?'

This was Dr. John Hunter, popularly known as Jack among the 'resurrection men' upon whom he depended for corpses to dissect. He lived at 31 Golden Square (fashionable, but handy to the Pestfield) when Blake was a boy, and ran there private classes in anatomy and operative surgery for more than twenty pupils. He had first refusal of all animals dying in the Tower or in other menageries. In 1783 Hunter was living in Leicester Square close by, where he rose at 5 a.m. to get to work in his museum and demonstration theatre. He was dedicated, unfeeling and overbearing—as Blake portrays him.

The writing of *An Island in the Moon* has an uncommitted tone rare in Blake. The satire does not require his anger or his pity (even at such heartless surgery), merely his harsh exposure. The characters reveal themselves violently; the effect is strained and boisterous, and shows Quid the Cynic, supposedly Blake himself, enjoying the company he is pillorying, and sharing its envy—certainly sharing the envy of Miss Gittipin for comforts and display beyond her purse, as she complains:

> There they go in Post-chaises to Vauxhall and Ranelagh, and I hardly know what a coach is, except when I go to Mr. Jacko's—he knows what riding is, and his wife is the most agreeable woman—you hardly know she has a tongue in her head. And he is the funniest fellow, and I do believe he'll go in partnership with his master, and they have black servants lodge at their house. I never saw such a place in my life. He says he has six and twenty rooms in his house, and I believe it, and he is not such a liar as Quid thinks he is (but he is always envying).

Mr. Jacko (because he resembled Jacko the famous performing monkey) was Richard Cosway, seventeen years Blake's senior, who had worked his way through drawing school by fetching and carrying, and had later taught at Pars's Drawing School which Blake attended. There Cosway had done shameless miniatures for snuff-box lids to suit the taste of the dandies. By 1771 the ragged boy had become a full Academician. Ten years later he married the Italian daughter of an Irishman who ran an inn at Leghorn, and, being socially alert, kept her in seclusion till she had learnt to speak and behave as the English—which accounts for Miss Gittipin's remark about her quietness.

In 1784, just before Blake wrote of him, he moved from Berkeley Street to Schomberg House, Pall Mall, which certainly had twenty-six rooms, as Jacko said; but he only lived in the central part, so Quid and Jacko were both right. Miss Gittipin's remark that she had 'never seen such a place' in her life is understandable. Cosway had taken the house over from James Graham, a quack doctor who had only in 1783 redecorated 'the suite of apartments in this Elysian Palace' in 'celestial soul-transporting' style as a 'Temple of Health and Hymen'. The west wing housed

Thomas Gainsborough himself, who 'blotted and blurred', according to Blake, and 'divided all the English world' with Reynolds.

Cosway, 'full dressed in his sword and bag with a small three-cornered hat on the top of his powdered *toupé* and a mulberry silk coat profusely embroidered with strawberries', is said to have earned £10,000 a year from the Prince of Wales who (no less) is the 'master' Miss Gittipin mentions. Maria Cosway's Sunday evening concerts were so fashionable that Pall Mall was jammed with carriages, and so close was Jacko to the throne that he had a private way from his house to Carlton Palace Gardens.

Cosway was a follower of Swedenborg, turned to mysticism later in life, claimed to have conversations with the Virgin Mary as she sat for him, and died only six years before Blake, another one-time Swedenborgian and mystic. Blake also held communion with the dead and saw their visionary forms—but under the creative control of his imagination. In a curiously warped, forbidding way, Cosway's career reflects what Blake might have been, had he caught the fashion with his print shop in 1784, as he so nearly did. But it was Jacko the monkey, not Quid, who 'succeeded'.

It is not very important that we should be able to identify precisely this or that character in *An Island in the Moon*. Jack Tearguts is John Hunter; but he could as well have been the elder brother, William Hunter, who ran the Anatomical Theatre (with its own burial ground) in Great Windmill Street, or Joshua Brookes the anatomist who gave lectures across the bodies of criminals in Blenheim Street. And Inflammable Gass the Wind-finder, probably Joseph Priestley, could as well have been Henry Cavendish himself, who was working on arsenic in 1784 at 13 Great Marlborough Street, near Broad Street, and was a greater authority on 'inflammable gas' than Priestley.

The point is that Blake has not chosen odd company. The characters may be accepted under their pseudonyms as representative, in their manners, behaviour and preoccupations, of many around Broad Street in the exaggerated peace of the mid '80s. Blake for these few years was much among company, which for him was enjoyable when it was eccentric, enquiring, irreverent and brash; and he liked it sardonic when aspirations exploded in its face. It is important, because this is Blake (unlikely as it may seem) at the time he wrote *Songs of Innocence*. It should warn us not to read the *Songs* ingenuously.

ii

Songs of Innocence was the first of Blake's poetical works to be published by his process of 'illuminated printing'—relief etching on copper followed by hand-tinting in water-colour. The earliest issue bears the date on the title-page 1789, though all the plates may not have been finished by that year. In 1794 Blake issued the combined volume *Songs of Innocence and of Experience Shewing the Two Contrary States of the Human Soul*.

Three of the *Songs of Innocence*—*Holy Thursday, The Little Boy Lost* and *Nurse's Song*—were written for *An Island in the Moon*, where they appear in a satirical context. This has led some critics to read all the *Songs of Innocence* as satirical, a view that must be discussed. On the other hand, the *Songs* are sometimes seen as more or less emotive recollections by Blake of his own childhood experiences. But it is difficult to see how a poem like *Nurse's Song* can be such a recollection *and* composed for *An Island in the Moon*. Moreover, by the time he was engraving *Songs of Innocence*, Blake had already written some of the contrary poems of Experience. This all implies a scheme of work independent of nostalgic recollections of his childhood.

Further, as he wrote *Songs of Innocence* Blake was also writing *Thel*, a poem that describes retreat from Experience, rather than true Innocence, and *Tiriel*, a book he never engraved which is loaded with the effects of superstition. So the last thing we can expect from *Songs of Innocence* is naïvety.

In *Songs of Innocence* two threadbare 18th-century literary fashions come together and are transformed. The contemporary pastoral was a highly self-conscious recollection of the age-old tradition of nymphs and swains and was sophisticated into a pretence at simplicity that was often salacious, always shallow and invariably boring. The cultivated, recognisably expected manner of writing of the countryside was so ordinary that wherever one turns in 18th-century poetry it is inescapable. The variations on the theme of 'innocence'—innocent pleasure, innocent seduction, innocent submission, even innocent rape in groves and shades 'where sporting lambkins play', were endlessly repetitive. There was one way, and one only, of looking at the country, which enabled the poet to look without seeing, and concealed reality; it was a kind of automatic poetry, established and revered in the illustrious example of Milton. But Milton was a hundred degenerating years away.

Moreover, the pastoral lawns had been usurped by the establishment and invaded by the town rakes. The 'simplicity' of pastoral life (labour, country poverty, hunger and discomfort being quite discounted) was presented as a facile alternative to the cares of city and court. In this fictional landscape indulgence was always available beneath skies that never glowered, with shepherdesses who acknowledged the rules of the game—that the only permitted reticence was a provocative coyness. And yet alongside all this ran an inevitably well-bred, powdered morality.

The commonplace language of the verse—'beauteous maid', 'souls on fire', 'charming fair', 'flowery mead', 'gentle shepherds', 'tender flocks'—disarms thought and elevates the writing with appropriate tone. And at times the pastoral and the power of the establishment run with facility together, when 'swains, and princely merchants, aid the verse',

> . . . while the Supreme accounts
> Well of the faithful shepherd, ranked alike
> With King and priest.

THE FLEECE I, 672–4

So the pastoral had become formality—a form for the suggestive lyric or the polite concealment of the countryside reality of toil. And often the ready association of careful shepherd and pastoral king led the poet's pen into an almost ritual sequence of ideas. So James Thomson, in one of the most widely approved and influential of all 18th-century poems, told how he watched

> Where sits the shepherd on the grassy turf,
> Inhaling, healthful, the descending sun.
> Around him feeds his many-bleating flock,
> Of various cadence; and his sportive lambs,
> This way and that convolved, in friskful glee,
> Their frolics play.

A mere six lines farther on he is contemplating Britain:

> . . . ere yet she grew
> To this deep-laid indissoluble state,
> Where wealth and commerce lift their golden heads;
> And o'er our labours, liberty and law
> Impartial watch; the wonder of the world!
>
> THE SEASONS, SPRING, 830–45

Even pastoral landscapes gave shelter with the familiar reassurances.

Alongside this convention, and blending with it at times, was the 18th-century profitable and pious trade in moral books for children. These could be prose or verse—it made little difference to the tone, impeccably polite, admonitory, and tediously improving.

The *genre* had a long pedigree, going back to Bunyan's *Book for Boys and Girls* (1686) and Isaac Watts's *Divine Songs for the Use of Children* (1715). As John Gay wrote in *Fables* (1727):

> . . . every object of creation
> Can furnish hints to contemplation,
> And from the most minute and mean
> A virtuous mind can morals glean.

We have never been at a loss for adults of 'virtuous mind' prepared to glean morals for the children's 'improvement'; and since it is the adult who buys the book for a child, and all adults wish children to be 'improved', commercial success was assured. In these books 'designed for the amusement and instruction of

68

youth', the narrative leads inevitably to the admonition, and the justice of the admonition is, sooner or later, always acknowledged. In this 'rich treasury of knowledge and moral instruction', 'the great truths of morality and religion' had been often and, it was claimed, 'so successfully enforced, that little, if anything, remains to be said on those subjects'. But this did not stop the 'ingenious writers of the present age' incessantly repeating what little remained.

Among these 'ingenious writers' was Mrs. Anne Barbauld, who kept a school in Sussex, spent the vacations in London and was often at the house of Joseph Johnson, the publisher of Blake's *The French Revolution*. Blake certainly knew her book *Hymns in Prose for Children* (1781), must have known the author herself, and very likely (as David Erdman suggests) used her as the original for Mrs. Nannicantipot in *An Island in the Moon*, where her song follows that of Obtuse Angle, who sings at Miss Gittipin's request:

> Upon a Holy Thursday, their innocent faces clean,
> The children walking two and two in grey and blue and green,
> Grey headed beadles walked before with wands as white as snow,
> Till into the high dome of Paul's, they like Thames' waters flow.
>
> Oh what a multitude they seemed, these flowers of London town,
> Seated in companies they sit with radiance all their own.
> The hum of multitudes were there but multitudes of lambs,
> Thousands of little boys and girls raising their innocent hands.
>
> Then like a mighty wind they raise to heaven the voice of song,
> Or like harmonious thunderings the seats of heaven among.
> Beneath them sit the reverend men, the guardians of the poor.
> Then cherish pity lest you drive an angel from your door.

'After this', Blake writes, 'they all sat silent for a quarter of an hour. Mrs. Nannicantipot said, "it puts me in mind of my mother's song"':

> When the tongues of children are heard on the green,
> And laughing is heard on the hill,
> My heart is at rest within my breast,
> And everything else is still.

Then come home, my children, the sun is gone down,
And the dews of night arise,
Come, come, leave off play, and let us away,
Till the morning appears in the skies.

No, no, let us play, for it is yet day
And we cannot go to sleep;
Besides, in the sky the little birds fly,
And the meadows are covered with sheep.

Well, well, go and play till the light fades away,
And then go home to bed.
The little ones leaped and shouted and laughed
And all the hills echoed.

With only minor changes, Blake used both these songs, as *Holy Thursday* and *Nurse's Song*, in *Songs of Innocence*. Separated by a reverential silence of fifteen minutes, they are clearly intended as mocking in their original context. From this it is sometimes argued that the poems are satirical in *Songs of Innocence*, and that many other *Songs* are to be read as satire, especially *The Chimney Sweeper*, which is otherwise seen as difficult to reconcile to the theme of Innocence. If one takes this view, it is possible to relate it to Blake's attitude, way of life and choice of company about the time when the *Songs* were written. However, for me *Songs of Innocence* is not intended satirically. The reader suspects nothing ironic in the text itself until the background to the book suggests it may be there.

We have seen how a change of context can change the meaning of a word, and how a sentence, only slightly qualified, can bring quite different responses from a reader. So it is the context of satire, the fact that the singers are at 'another merry meeting at the house of Steelyard the Lawgiver', that determines our response to the two songs in *An Island in the Moon*. Once they appear in *Songs of Innocence* the poems around them qualify their meaning, by directing the frame of mind in which we read them.

Jeremiah Seed wrote in 1743: 'In a word, public worship is the great instrument of securing a sense of God's providence and of a world to come; and a sense of God's providence and a world to come is the great basis of all social and private duties.' This justification of church-going, based on order in society, was commonplace in the century, and Blake deals brusquely with it in *An Island in the Moon*. There the lines *Upon a Holy Thursday* point at the convenient inculcation of correct attitudes in the annual congregation of charity schools. They marched 'two and two' by parishes, 4,500 children and 7,500 others, to the specially erected wooden galleries in St. Paul's, scrubbed and bright in their distinctive uniforms, in a demonstration of the success of English philanthropy and social welfare. As Blake says, let us all sit 'silent for a quarter of an hour' in contemplating the magnitude of these good works. But the impetus of *Songs of Innocence* gives no time for silent contemplation of *Holy Thursday*. And released from the house of Steelyard the Lawgiver, and set in the clear air of *Songs of Innocence*, this great poem (perhaps never a great *satirical* poem) takes on a new dimension.

Similarly, Mrs. Nannicantipot's mother's song may be ironic at the expense of Mrs. Anna Barbauld's 'improving' books for the young; but the same poem as *Nurse's Song* carries no hint of irony. Moreover, it seems to me that any satirical implications read into these (and other) poems in *Songs of Innocence* deprive the 'contrary' poems Blake wrote in *Songs of Experience* of their devastating effect.

iii

We may observe, that a disregard to all authority is the distinguishing character of the age. Children are undutiful to parents, servants are disobedient to their masters, and subjects to those that are set over them. And can they wonder at it, who seldom or never recognise in the most open and conspicuous manner, the authority of that Being, in whom all authority, in the last link of the chain, terminates; and from whom it must be derived to Governors, Parents and Masters.

That, again, is Jeremiah Seed, discoursing on 'several important subjects'. But it could be any sermon, and is the basis upon which the books approved by adults for the young were devised. If the countryside was described in such books it was inevitably polite, cultivated and carefully hedged. Children were given 'tasks', accepted them with subservient alacrity, and finished them with diligence. They acknowledged the wisdom of clergy, and they admitted their obligation to parent and guardian. Authority was rarely absent. Even animals were endowed with gratitude to their creator, and 'His all-seeing eye' was inescapable. Beside the constricting moral and the landscape lying beneath mankind's controlling hand, in these books eternity itself is bound in hours and days. The years to manhood are measured and days are doled out to youth in expectation of obedient conformity.

In this 'age of equal refinement and corruption of manners, when systems of education and seduction go hand in hand; when religion itself compounds with fashion', wrote Blake's friend, Henry Fuseli, 'reason and fancy have exhausted their stores of argument and imagery . . . animate and inanimate nature . . . have lent their real and supposed analogies . . . so often to emblematic purposes, that instruction has become stale and attention callous'. (Preface to *The Grave*, by Robert Blair.)

Fuseli puts the dilemma quite clearly. Examples of the 'real and supposed analogies' devised along the broad lane of morality, are legion:

> . . . birds sung in the hedge which enclosed the meadow; all was gay and seemed to laugh with joy. Charles laughed too, and catching the Curate's hand, he said, what a beautiful place! if my father and mother were here I should never wish to leave it while I lived.
>
> Then the Curate gave each of the children their task . . . little Caroline had a bed to weed . . .
>
> ELEMENTS OF MORALITY, FOR THE USE OF CHILDREN, C. G. SALZMANN (1790), 42–3

In *Songs of Innocence* the scene is no longer a locality for a lesson, but absorbed into the thought. In Innocence no hedges enclose the meadows, dividing, separating man from neighbour; division is an aspect of Experience. Innocent nature does not 'seem' to laugh; it *laughs*—

> When the green woods laugh with the voice of joy,
> And the dimpling stream runs laughing by,
> And the air does laugh with our merry wit,
> And the green hill laughs with the noise of it.

—in a universal identity of joy only expressible in these words. Morality is irrelevant, and Blake realises the unequivocal nature of laughter.

There is no question in Innocence of observing nature from outside; there are no polite expressions at the beauty of landscape. In Blake's Innocence the parents and aged are not sentimentally recollected, but involved in the delight. Innocence is unanswerable. In Innocence the children never use phrases like 'while I lived', speaking with adult voices; future and past meet in an eternal present—time undivided. When the sun rises, they wake, when light fades, they sleep. The authoritative injunction of the nurse in *Nurse's Song* yields to the natural logic of light and dark.

So in *Songs of Innocence* the landscape, together with all life in it, becomes a symbol realising a concept. It is hardly possible to state what that concept is, except in the words Blake used. But we sense that *Songs of Innocence* is relevant today because the concepts it gainsays (the moral righteousness, the assumption of adult superiority, the directives, the false attitudes, the 'sanctity' of labour, the cherishing of inhibitions) still fashion the Experience of our own society. So the book is gloriously unique in the concessions it refuses to make.

'Innocence,' Blake wrote much later, 'dwells with wisdom, but never with ignorance.' Moreover, it had to be '*organised* Innocence', otherwise there was no such thing. It is as if for a brief few years when the nation was at peace, Blake could accept the possibility of a social organism, rather than a social structure, arising from the humanitarian and philanthropic ideas of his day. And these few years coincided with the beginning of his married life. Poems on Experience were already occupying his mind, and indeed written, and he was aware of evil; but he was able to see Innocence as an attainable ideal, without the conflict later associated inevitably with the creation of Jerusalem in 'England's green and pleasant land'.

At about this time Blake liberally annotated a book called Lavater's *Aphorisms*, translated by Fuseli and issued in 1788. Blake's notes are often read as a key to his thought during the writing of *Songs of Innocence*. But perhaps most important of all is the fact that Blake made no comment at all on these two aphorisms:

> no. 280   He who seeks to embitter innocent pleasure
> has a cancer in his heart.
>
> no. 495   The cruelty of the effeminate is more
> dreadful than that of the hardy.

Blake wrote hundreds of lines on those two themes, and yet, only two or three years before he wrote *My Pretty Rose-tree*, his mind was so clear of these later obsessive questions that his eye simply failed to see these aphorisms. In *Songs of Innocence* Blake is not recollecting his childhood walks or writing a phantasy, but looking at society no less surely than in *Songs of Experience*, where personal emotions (envy, malice, suspicion) are involved, and privacy is part of the theme. In *Songs of Innocence* his task was more difficult, however, since the only language at his disposal was inevitably the language of Experience. Not only had he to avoid the divisive and authoritative assumptions of the children's moralists, but also the suggestive and polished inanities of commonplace pastoral verse.

While the ordinary 18th-century pastoral was an idealisation of ignorance, a formal avoidance of unpleasant truth, the idealised landscape in *Songs of Innocence* is based upon an observation of pastoral reality among evils readily acknowledged. Almost from the beginning, The Foundling Hospital had boarded out children under three years old with foster parents in the country, a practice made general by Act of Parliament in 1767. But Blake's parish of St. James had for some years been sending destitute

74

children to the country, especially to cottagers at Wimbledon, just beyond Battersea where Blake met and married his wife.

More immediately, in 1782 the parish of St. James acquired an old riding school in King Street, known as Foubert's Academy, and spent over £7,000 repairing it as a School of Industry, to house over two hundred children. The older children were moved here from the workhouse behind Blake's house, and the practice of sending the younger children to nurse at Wimbledon was extended. So successful and enlightened for its age was this treatment that only six children died in five years. The average mortality among pauper children in workhouses was one in two.

The effect of this on Blake's imagination needs no emphasis. Here is 'organised Innocence' based upon wisdom. All the country to the south of the Thames, 'the lovely hills of Camberwell', 'the fields of corn at Peckham Rye', the pastures of Stockwell, Clapham, Dulwich and Denmark Hill, were familiar to Blake; it was the nearest unspoilt open countryside to Westminster, Hampstead being sophisticated. We may even, if we like, give a location to 'the mire' and 'the lonely fen' in *The Little Boy Lost* and *Found*, along the common watercourse of Vauxhall Creek, or about Rush Common and Water Lane to the east of Brixton Hill.

It seems beyond question that Wimbledon Common and the arc of hills just south of the Thames are the visual location of *Songs of Innocence*, and the unqualified enlightenment of putting children under six out with country nurses is the visionary organisation that stimulated Blake to write them. So when Blake transferred *When the voices of children are heard on the green* from Mrs. Nannicantipot to *Songs of Innocence* he called it *Nurse's Song*—precisely what it is, with Wimbledon Common in mind. His own childhood is irrelevant.

iv

In some of the *Songs* the lamb is simply a part of the landscape of Innocence, in common with the children, birds and streams. But in *The Shepherd* the familiar Christian symbolism of shepherd and lamb is clear. The shepherd suggests God, and the ewe and the lamb suggest mother and child. In *The Lamb* the animal is at first the symbol of God's created Innocence, and a demonstration of His care for creatures of earth. So divine care is reflected in the social practice of sending poor infants to the country. Then by a beautiful turning of the poem, the 'Lamb of God' symbol identifies Jesus in Innocence, and the whole pastoral tenderness is given a symbolic Christian identity. This God is not the God of retribution, but identified in the child and the lamb He has created and is protecting. The poem closes in an awareness of divine, human and pastoral unity;

> I a child and thou a lamb,
> We are called by his name.

In *Night*, a poem hardly written with a 'rural pen' in its developing symbolism, Blake takes this matter of 'organised Innocence' a stage further. The universe of night is transformed in a phrase to an arbour of sleep, where bird, child, blossom and beast are indivisibly protected by 'angels bright'. But they represent no divine providence that at the wave of a wand can confer inviolability to death. 'When wolves and tigers howl for prey,' there are sometimes victims. The angels protect their flock by pitying the aggressor, and if pity fails to quench the thirst for blood in feral nature, heaven becomes the victims' home.

This is the crucial poem in *Songs of Innocence*. Reality is faced quite squarely. The angels are ministering to their charges, as are the nurses. The pastoral platitude of inevitable survival is reversed in a symbolic acceptance of the presence of cruelty and death in Innocence; but death is not a threat, or a punishment, or a consequence of sin (as it is made in Experience), but a transition to 'new worlds'. And the after-life is not at this stage a hypocritical reassurance. The innocent need no reassuring. There is an illuminating contrast between *Night* and *The Little Girl Lost* and *The Little Girl Found*, two poems that Blake originally wrote for *Songs of Innocence*, and later rightly transferred to *Songs of*

76

Experience. Death comes in *Night*, but in the poems of Experience the power of chastity rather than innocence leads to the benevolence of royal protection in a lonely, apparently inviolable, seclusion of meaningless permanence. This Experience is much closer to the specious pastoral fashion than Blake's Innocence.

At the end of the fourth stanza of *Night*, the 'new worlds' beyond death are contemplated:

> And there the lion's ruddy eyes
> Shall flow with tears of gold,
> And pitying the tender cries,
> And walking round the fold,
> Saying 'Wrath by his meekness,
> And by his health, sickness
> Is driven away
> From our immortal day.'

The regal lion weeps in pity, the tyrant succumbs to the meek, and daylight is everlasting. And this incorruptible God drives away disease; in Experience the god worshipped in the churches wields the pestilence.

In *Songs of Innocence* the notion of 'new worlds' after death is acceptable, as it is not tendentious and a polite fiction. These 'new worlds' are simply a continuum into eternity of the state of 'organised Innocence' on earth. *Night* is not a dream-sequence; once again, it seems to me to arise from an observed reality, the brief glimpse of a divine ideal fixed in time among the pauper children in the country, rescued by an exercise of true Christian charity from the sickness of the workhouse. The meaning of the poem opens out if it is read as a symbolic restatement of this undertaking, until even the lion, the symbol of supreme temporal power, could lie down with the lamb, and 'guard o'er the fold'. When he signed that Act of Parliament (7 George III c 39), even King George III was for once enlightened.

Unless we read *Night* in this way, *The Chimney Sweeper* and *Holy Thursday* can only be either meaningless, or satirical, or not true Songs of Innocence. These poems come nearest, some would say too dangerously near, to reflecting the moral tone of the writers of 'prose and verse for children'. And in both cases the children are seen in London, not in the landscape of Innocence.

The annual charity school service in St. Paul's was valued as a demonstration of the success of philanthropy, and the impressive muster of school colours was bright and reassuring in its obedient formality. The horror of the reality was concealed. But Blake is not now neglecting the horror, which he knew only too well, nor subscribing to facile conscience-salving. In *Songs of Innocence* the poem is not followed by a pious silence, in itself satirical; and the new context only highlights the focus in the poem, which is all upon the children. The beadles with their wands are no more than ushers to colourful innocence. The children dominate, and symbolise Innocence, while the social unity that typifies the pastoral Songs is momentarily caught in St. Paul's. The children with 'a radiance all their own' possess the occasion and the imagination as completely as they control the reactions in *Nurse's Song* or *The Echoing Green*. Innocence transforms occasions.

In *The Chimney Sweeper* the speaker seems perilously close to the pious comforter as he begins:

> When my mother died I was very young,
> And my father sold me while yet my tongue
> Could scarcely cry ''weep! 'weep! 'weep! 'weep!'
> So your chimneys I sweep, and in soot I sleep.

> There's little Tom Dacre who cried when his head,
> That curled like a lamb's back, was shaved. So I said
> 'Hush, Tom! never mind it, for when your head's bare
> You know that the soot cannot spoil your white hair.'

Blake again has his eye firmly on reality. Tom Dacre, consoled by this uncommonly philosophical infant, is himself a foundling. In Westminster the Lady Ann Dacre's Alms Houses ('called Emanuel College') admitted ten poor men and women, provided they could 'say the creed and ten commandments in English', 'each of whom has liberty to bring up one poor child'. So Tom Dacre is a foundling's name, and his foster-parent has cashed his privilege by selling the boy to a master sweep. This was the most degrading of all apprenticeships—worse than the sea and the milk sellers. But in 1788 an Act of Parliament limited the hours of work, and forbade the employment of children under eight years old, and in chimneys that were on fire. So when Blake wrote the poem the way to reform seemed clear. He was not to know then that this Act (unlike the Act of 1767 governing children sent to the country) was to remain a dead-letter.

If we remember, which may be difficult, that the speaker in the second stanza is another child, the words of solace take on an infant sympathy, which is accepted and is successful in its reassurance. The consequent dream Tom enjoys promises after death a transformation to eternal fields. This is easier to reconcile with Innocence than the final admonition:

> And the angel told Tom, if he'd be a good boy,
> He'd have God for his father, and never want joy.

> And so Tom awoke, and we rose in the dark,
> And got with our bags and our brushes to work.
> Though the morning was cold, Tom was happy and warm;
> So if all do their duty they need not fear harm.

In *Holy Thursday* the Innocence shines from a setting of social righteousness. In *The Chimney Sweeper* the Innocence transcends the evil in which it is set, conquering, as it were, by submission. It is the philosophy behind the poem *Night* applied to the Westminster streets. And again, it is the absolute unsuspecting acceptance of assurances, the unqualified trust, that makes *The Chimney Sweeper* a poem of Innocence. Innocence here, as in the country, is a state of mind.

Both here and in *Holy Thursday*, Blake's point is the inviolability of Innocence, a spiritual, rather than physical, state, immune to moral righteousness. *The Chimney Sweeper* is a disturbing poem in the dangerous course it runs. And what I find most difficult to reconcile with Innocence is not the appalling occupation and the visionary promise, but the divisive element of duty and obedience. At first it seems that the angel has simply learnt his platitudes too well, and the narrator is too good a child to be true. At a second thought it seems perhaps that the speakers' identities make all the difference, as such voices, angelic and infant, cannot betray—at least, not yet. The last verse is trite, until we remember that it is spoken by an apprentice sweep, which makes the third line as factual as the first two. And this makes the last two lines disturbing. Innocence is not easy.

v

In three Songs, *A Dream*, and *The Little Boy Lost* and *Found*, Blake turns to the mystical background of Innocence. Children who are lost and bewildered are brought to safety by miraculous intervention. In these poems, with their uneasy and deceptive landscape of tangled spray, mist, the dews of night, lonely fens and dales, through which a weary, benighted traveller wanders, we sense that Innocence is already threatened.

About 1789 Blake wrote *Tiriel*, in which the 'laws of Har', who never grows from childishness, and the oppression of Tiriel, who in senility and dotage clings to authority, end 'together in a curse', and the questions of Experience are asked:

> Why is one law given to the lion and the patient ox,
> And why men bound beneath the heavens in reptile form,
> A worm of sixty winters creeping on the dusky ground.
> The child springs from the womb. The father ready stands to form
> The infant head, while the mother idle plays with her dog on her
>   couch.
> The young bosom is cold for lack of mother's nourishment and
>   milk,

until the infant walks 'in sorrow, compelled to number footsteps Upon the sand' (*Tiriel*, 8).

The solace of Har and Heva, the offspring of Tiriel, are 'the

pleasant gardens of Har', where their mother tends them even
in age, and they indulge in affected simplicity:

> And Har and Heva like two children sat beneath the Oak.
> Mnetha, now aged, waited on them, and brought them food and
>   clothing.
> But they were as the shadow of Har, and as the years forgotten;
> Playing with flowers and running after birds they spent the day,
> And in the night like infants slept, delighted with infant dreams.
>
> TIRIEL, 2

Tiriel deals in harsh measure with senile tyranny, and Har and
Heva, the children of such tyranny, console themselves with
barren diversions, clinging to a thoughtless existence, and
avoiding a life of Experience. The geographical location suggest-
ing the vale and gardens of Har was surely Vauxhall Gardens,
in the Vale of Lambeth on the road to Battersea. The fashionable
walks at Vauxhall were 'well planted with lofty trees that form a
delightful shade, with woodbines and underwoods, which fur-
nish a safe asylum for the birds'; though Sir Roger de Coverley
remarked that he would have liked the gardens better 'if there
were more nightingales and fewer strumpets'.

The Book of Thel is also dated 1789, and Thel, who is the
'virgin of the skies', conscious and yet afraid of her transient
nature, is also 'mistress of the vales of Har', so close to, yet so far
from, the hills of Innocence. In her encounters with the most
humble aspects of creation, she is brought up against the instinctive and disinterested participation in life that we have seen
realised in Innocence, and she draws back in fear. She acknow-
ledges that, even for the Worm, the essence of life is a relationship
of interdependence, and at the same time laments her own
separate and uncommitted nature. She 'wishes but acts not'.
Blake is not yet attacking the assumptions that perpetuated the
misery of social division, but pitying the desolation of spirit in a
being isolated from life by her fear of life, and seeking an
illusory fulfilment in her benevolent, anxious aloofness. Thel only
touches life at a distance. She is at once afraid and regretful:

For I walk through the vales of Har and smell the sweetest flowers,
But I feed not the little flowers. I hear the warbling birds,
But I feed not the warbling birds; they fly and seek their food.
But Thel delights in these no more, because I fade away;
And all shall say, 'Without a use this shining woman lived,
Or did she only live to be the food of worms?'

THEL II

The implications of the long running lines in *The Book of Thel*, pervaded with a strangely gentle, questioning menace, are clearly still with us today. And our own age still echoes the terrifying crescendo of questions that drives Thel back to the refuge of the vales of Har. With these questions Blake brings us to the edge of Experience, and his voice sounds ominously close across two hundred years:

Why cannot the ear be closed to its own destruction?
Or the glistening eye to the poison of a smile?
Why are eyelids stored with arrows ready drawn
Where a thousand fighting men in ambush lie?
Or an eye of gifts and graces showering fruits and coined gold?
Why a tongue impressed with honey from every wind?
Why an ear, a whirlpool fierce to draw creation in?
Why a nostril wide inhaling terror, trembling and affright?
Why a tender curb upon the youthful burning boy?
Why a little curtain of flesh on the bed of our desire?

THEL IV

6

Visions and Revolution

i

1788 was the centenary of an English revolution, a fact that had not escaped the Republican friends of Blake. In the summer of 1789 Paris was behind barricades, and on July 14 the Bastille was raided. Three years later France was a Republic, and during these years the proposition that 'men are born and remain free and equal in rights' seemed a substantial promise to Blake's Republican friends, even in England under George III.

Blake's sympathies were all with the Republicans. For him the fires of revolt would destroy the ancient tyranny of priest and king to reveal mankind in freedom. And he would rejoice in a London ablaze with revolution.

Fires were a frequent sight in London, but two conflagrations especially, both in the parish of St. James, could have provided the visual stimulus to the poet's imagination, and both could be seen as symbolic because of royal associations.

On June 17, 1789, a few weeks before the Bastille fell, at ten o'clock at night the roof of the King's Theatre, Haymarket, seemed to burst into flame in an instant, and with incredible speed the whole theatre was gutted. That was five minutes' walk from Poland Street. Even more spectacularly, a few yards from Blake's house, the Pantheon itself went up in flames in the small hours of Saturday, January 14, 1792. The cold night wind roared into the building, until 'this finest of modern temples, with its scaglioli columns' was enveloped in flame. The vast damask curtains were blown like flags till they caught fire, the chandeliers whirled and fell, and a pillar of fire burst through the dome of the building. So great was the blaze that James Wyatt, the architect who had converted the Pantheon for use as an opera house (called again, prophetically, the King's Theatre), saw the glow in the sky when he was crossing Salisbury Plain in a post-chaise, and thought all London was on fire. The wild animals chained in the menagerie in the garden of Joshua Brookes, the anatomist, at the back of the Pantheon, were panic-stricken by the fire, and the mob, seeing them through the railings, threatened to ransack the house.

The whole situation—the temple-like building with its columns and arches, the royal associations, the night wind whipping the flames, the pillar of fire, the waving banners of the curtains, the angry mob, and the terrified animals attending on death in a garden among 'large masses of the Rock of Gibraltar' —the whole scene could hardly be more effective.

Blake often uses violent flames as a symbol of revolution, the forces of reaction being associated with dull, sullen, smouldering fire. Again, this symbolism seems to have a visual basis in contemporary London. And at a metaphysical level, the forces of revolt are Satanic, supported by the inferno of hell's flames, against the organised and repressive resistance of king and priest, seen as angelic orders. Again, all this has a contemporary justification. The French themselves commonly associated the violent Revolution with the revolt of Satan. For instance, in the atrocious Vendéan War that followed the execution of Louis XVI in 1793, the revolutionary forces led by Thurreau against the priests and royalist population in the cliff-bound ranges of Western France were called 'infernal columns'. Their enemies were armed by sea from England.

Between 1790 and the Vendéan War Blake wrote *The Marriage of Heaven and Hell*. This is an ironic prophecy and a call to question established values. It proclaims the possibility of redemption from oppression in a release of energy, desire and will. It denies the supremacy of reason, and declares that

> Those who restrain desire, do so because theirs is weak enough to be restrained; and the restrainer or reason usurps its place and governs the unwilling.

And being restrained it by degrees becomes passive till it is only the shadow of desire.

Such lines as these have led to the easy misunderstanding that Blake advocated free love. And many of the Proverbs of Hell in *The Marriage* seem to say as much in a facile reading. But the reading has to be incredibly facile. The last thing Blake advocated was promiscuity, which implies self-indulgence. Moreover, he expressly blamed the code of Urizen for the prevalence of prostitution. And there is always a clear implication of intellectual and spiritual freedom behind his arguments which exalt desire and the will. Indeed, the release and fulfilment of desire, innocent and open to the daylight, always symbolises the fight for spiritual and intellectual enfranchisement.

When we read the Proverbs of Hell we are faced once more with the challenge that questions our assumptions:

> He who desires but acts not, breeds pestilence.
> Prisons are built with stones of Law, brothels with bricks of Religion.
> One thought fills immensity.
> As the caterpillar chooses the fairest leaves to lay her eggs on, so the priest lays his curse on the fairest joys.
> To create a little flower is the labour of ages.
> Sooner murder an infant in its cradle than nurse unacted desires.

The essential philosophy is that 'everything that lives is holy', and the identity of each living creature should be accepted as inviolable:

> How do you know but every bird that cuts the airy way,
> Is an immense world of delight, closed by your senses five?

Blake demands a complete, and if necessary violent, rejection of all that has inhibited life in mankind. But this could not be further from free love (as we use the phrase) in furtive concealment and with a degradation of perception.

> If the doors of perception were cleansed everything would appear to man as it is, infinite.
> For man has closed himself up, till he sees all things through narrow chinks of his cavern.

Blake prefaced *The Marriage* with an *Argument*:

Rintrah roars and shakes his fires in the burdened air;
Hungry clouds swag on the deep.

Once meek, and in a perilous path,
The just man keeps his course along
The vale of death.
Roses are planted where thorns grow,
And on the barren heath
Sing the honey bees.

Then the perilous path was planted,
And a river and a spring
On every cliff and tomb;
And on the bleached bones
Red clay brought forth.

Till the villain left the paths of ease,
To walk in perilous paths, and drive
The just man into barren climes.

Now the sneaking serpent walks
In mild humility,
And the just man rages in the wilds
Where lions roam.

Rintrah roars and shakes his fires in the burdened air;
Hungry clouds swag on the deep.

Rintrah, whose regal identity is elaborated in *Europe*, clearly represents the ponderous forces of oppression. The transition from the roar of the royal lion to an atmosphere oppressive with thunder, storm, sullen fire and clouds sagging into the menacing oblivion of the ocean forms a symbolism of overwhelming tyranny. Against this, the 'just man' has arisen from meekness, walked the valley of death with resolution, planted the desert till the barren land bears fruit—and is betrayed. This fundamentally simple and disturbing poem radiates from an observation of a contemporary situation: in France, the Revolution; in London the self-seeking subservience of the clergy that ultimately delivered its victim to the law of iron and desolation. Generalising from these events, the poem is a pitiful epitaph on every lost endeavour, and a brief hint of the tragic waste of Experience.

ii

The Marriage of Heaven and Hell is difficult to date accurately, but in the front of one copy Blake wrote the cryptic words: 'Our End is come. Published June 5, 1793, by W. Blake Lambeth.' It is probable that *A Song of Liberty*, which anticipates *America* (1793) in many of its phrases, was written and appended to *The Marriage* in this or the previous year.

Blake has concealed his references too well for us to be certain if any one historical event motivated the poem. In the circumstances of the time, with a government sensitive to treason in the slightest remark, Blake could hardly be direct. Even so, the general terms of *A Song of Liberty* are unmistakable and outspoken.

By 1789 Washington had become the first President of the Republic, and the Americans had been free for some six years from imperial and commercial oppression. *A Song of Liberty* is a symbolic account of the spreading of this spirit of revolt to France, and a prophecy that England will follow, with an end to all oppression through universal resurgence.

The lines ring with elation at the prospect of the overthrow of imperial tyranny. It might be the victory of the French over Brunswick at Valmy in September 1792 that moved Blake, as David Erdman suggests. But this was not a rout such as *A Song of Liberty* describes, the 'starry hosts' of imperialism retreating unaccountably and in good order, Brunswick having decided that his position was untenable. Perhaps the execution of Louis XVI stimulated the poem; or it could simply be a sudden optimistic reflection on the way events appeared to be shaping. Certainly, the poem relates no one single engagement, and is at once retrospective and prophetic.

The first three verses recall the revolution in America. The 'eternal female' may be identified vaguely as the Church of Rome; but this identity should only be glanced at. She is also the female principle, later named Enitharmon, who dominates mankind under Urizen, armed with the powerful doctrine that 'woman's love is sin' and the irresistible weapon of alluring and reticent sexuality. This is all part of the tyranny. When this 'eternal female' groans at the beginning of *A Song of Liberty*, it expresses at once her misery and her birth pang. The offspring is to be 'the new born terror', later given the name Orc, the spirit of revolt.

So we have a number of threads running parallel in the poem, and we are not to cling to time as a series of years. The spirit of revolt is generated from within the ancient tyranny. Parallel with this run accounts of revolt against moral oppression at a personal level, against commercial greed, and against the organisation of religion. The time scale moves from a statement of the revolt in America (verses 1–3), through a call to Europe to follow this example (verses 3–6), partly fulfilled as France has already pulled down its dungeon, to an account of present conflict between revolutionary and counter-revolutionary forces (verses 7–16), the defeat of tyranny (verses 17–18) and the triumph of revolution (verses 19–20). Finally, there is the prophecy.

Of course, it is not as simple as that. Blake's poetry seems difficult at first, because he concentrates so many themes into a single statement, and comments simultaneously on the physical situation and the philosophy that shapes it. However, *A Song of Liberty* makes a good beginning. It may need a conscious effort before it ceases to seem odd or unnecessarily obscure. However, if we persist in reading it, gradually we begin to feel that the lines have an uncomfortable power. This is the crucial point. We may not like what we read, and we may not think it great poetry. But if we can acknowledge that Blake is communicating something that has not been heard before, we are ready for the challenging, terrifying, sometimes bewildering landscape of the prophetic books.

The Chorus at the end of *A Song of Liberty* relates the whole theme of political revolution to the human situation in Experience, where mankind is separated from his neighbour physically by walls and hedges, socially by class divisions, economically by possessions, and spiritually by creed and the worship of a deity whose priests perpetuate and justify this condition. In Experience, too, mankind's imagination is enclosed against the infinite within a roof. So although Blake asserted that 'where man is not, nature is barren', buildings, walls, gates, roofs and caverns are always symbols of constriction and repression—the antithesis to mankind's presence in the open pastures of Innocence.

So *A Song of Liberty*, dealing basically with events of national significance, brings us to the edge of everyday experience. This is the greatness of all Blake's shorter prophetic books, except *The French Revolution*.

iii

The French Revolution (1791) expresses Blake's complete commitment to Republican democracy at a time when monarchy still looked like surviving in France. It also provides a key to the symbolism of the later books, so clearly are symbols linked to recognisable conflicts and loyalties. It was also the last book Blake wrote for the normal processes of publishing. After this Blake etched his books himself, selling them to subscribers.

Though the publisher Joseph Johnson set up the book in page proof in 1791, it got no further and was never issued. It is pointless to speculate why the book was withdrawn, and we do not know whether Blake or Johnson was responsible. There was no breach between them (at least at a business level), as Blake continued to engrave for Johnson. The publisher was dilatory in his methods, and it may be that by 1791 it was felt that the speed of events had put Blake's narrative out of date. From Blake's point of view, the failure to publish was crucial. After this he was never faced with the essential discipline of communication other than to a few sympathetic but not always comprehending friends. Gradually his language became more and more cryptic.

The poem deals symbolically and freely with events from the

Council of State in June to the withdrawal of troops on July 15, 1789, the day after the fall of the Bastille. The action of this period is compressed into a single day; or rather, there is no sense of time at all. And Blake changes the course of events and introduces characters who have no historical existence. The nobles and others represent general or abstract ideas and movements. They are in this way something like the mythological figures in Blake's other books; the symbolism identifies them.

The Duke of Burgundy is invented to represent the nobility at its most arrogant and hostile to the people. He stood to speak (l. 83) as the 'ancientest peer' at 'the monarch's right hand'. As he rose 'the chamber became as a clouded sky', and 'clothed in flames of crimson'

> The fierce Duke hung over the Council; around him crowd, weeping in his burning robe,
> A bright cloud of infant souls.

Burgundy demands if the mowers 'from the Atlantic mountains' should be allowed to destroy 'all this great starry harvest of six thousand years'. The 'ancient forests of chivalry' should be preserved, not 'burnt for fuel' (l. 93), and to this end the nobles 'have gathered the starry hosts round this rebellious city' (l. 100). Burgundy opposes Necker, 'the hind of Geneva', temporarily identified with the populace, and Necker is driven from the kingdom (l. 114).

The Archbishop of Paris stands for the lofty privilege of the church, and in bidding his King listen to 'the terrors of heaven' (l. 128), he tells how he was visited in his midnight bower by 'an aged form, white as snow, hovering in mist', which whispered how

> groaning is heard in the abbeys, and God, so long worshipped, departs as a lamp
> Without oil. For a curse is heard hoarse through the land from a godless race
> Descending to beasts. They look downward and labour, and forget my holy law.

137–9

The Archbishop is afraid that 'Nobles and Clergy shall fail' and his 'cloud and vision be no more' (l. 143). So he tells the King that 'the command of heaven' is upon him, to shut up the Assembly 'in their final home', and turn 'this city of rebels' over to the militia:

> Let the Bastille devour
> These rebellious, seditious. Seal them up, O Anointed! in everlasting chains.
>
> 156–7

A vision of Henry IV makes the captains stand like 'men bound in chains', and 'the strong soldiers tremble', recalling the famous legend that Henry sought to end wars in Europe by an almost republican alliance of nations. Bourbon tries to rally 'this army of superstition'.

Historically, the Duke of Orleans had already set aside his title to join the people, and had acquired a new one, Monsieur Egalité. However, he appears here still ducal as the personification of liberal nobility, 'generous as mountains'. As he speaks, the Archbishop of Paris is reduced to a hissing serpent.

The Abbé de Sieyès, who had justified the Third Estate in a famous pamphlet in 1788, is made the revolutionary apologist by Blake, representing 'the voice of the people arising from valley and hill' (l. 206), against the ancient tyranny that has lasted since

> the heavens were sealed with a stone, and the terrible sun closed in an orb, and the moon
> Rent from the nations, and each star appointed for watchers of night,
> The millions of spirits immortal were bound in the ruins of sulphur, heaven
> To wander enslaved.
>
> 211–14

He foresees how the priest will no longer speak from 'his thunderous cloud', and devour the labour of the poor, but will put 'his hand to the plough', and how pestilence, oppression and war will end till

the happy earth sing in its course,
The mild peaceable nations be opened to heaven, and
men walk with their fathers in bliss.

236–7

The promise in this passage is of Innocence regained. But the promise is shattered by Burgundy, and Fayette calls the people to strife.

iv

In *Visions of the Daughters of Albion* (1793) Blake turns again to the contrast between Innocence and Experience. Urizen appears in this poem for the first time by name, and the rebellious denunciation of his repressive code is the major theme upon which the poem turns. The repression is at once spiritual, moral, economic, social and sexual. The symbolism is not obscure, and the unique triumph of the poem lies in the success with which Blake sustains the simultaneous relevance and interdependence of so many different aspects of the conflict between freedom and oppression.

Though the poem has long been recognised as a condemnation of the hypocritical code that established, justified and perpetuated social, personal and spiritual degradation, it was D. V. Erdman in *Blake: Prophet against Empire* who first noticed the initial dependence of the poem upon Blake's fury at the slave traffic.

In the early 1790s Blake was engaged by Joseph Johnson to work upon engravings for a book called *A Narrative of a five years' expedition against the revolted negroes . . . of South America*, by Captain J. G. Stedman, published in 1796. Among his engravings Blake had to illustrate the sufferings of the slaves, and their fortitude under prolonged torture.

Moreover, Stedman had married a slave named Joanna, but could not buy her freedom. In *Visions* Theotormon loves Oothoon, but cannot free her. Soon after his marriage, Stedman tried to intervene to stop the flagellation of a slave-girl who had 'refused to submit to the loathsome embraces of her detestable executioner'. Before Stedman's intervention, the girl had received two hundred lashes, and the overseer's reaction was to double the punishment. Stedman could only withdraw beyond earshot. Blake had the task of illustrating this incident, and it provides a revealing source for one thematic strand in *Visions*, with Theotormon as Stedman, Oothoon as both Joanna and the slave-girl, and Bromion as the overseer.

But of course *Visions* goes much deeper than mere outraged recollection, even on the slavery theme alone. Oothoon represents the desire, not only for the dignity of true affection, but for equality of emotional and spiritual experience. She claims recognition of her personal identity. Theotormon not only turns his back upon reality as did Stedman, reverencing the law of property more highly than humanity, but he also represents the ambivalent attitude of well-wishing men like Stedman, who for all his sensitiveness could not throw off entirely the inhibitions of his age. He was conscious that the natives did not share many failings of civilisation: 'A happy people I call them, whose errors are the errors of ignorance, and not the rooted depravity of a pretended civilisation and a spurious and mock Christianity.' Yet Stedman could not justify ending the slave trade, and this as well as the terrifying cruelty bit into Blake's imagination. We can match the depth of Blake's sense of tragedy and the scope of his appeal, against the unfeeling philanthropy of the age epitomised in Stedman's remark when he met a badly wounded man: 'I gave the miserable creature half a crown; and having agreed with Captain Orzinga upon the signal, we left this pest-house.'

While Theotormon represents the hesitant abolitionist, Bromion represents the established opponents of abolition, and their familiar arguments, that the 'abetters' of abolition would 'dry up the rivers of commerce' and undermine the structure of society. 'What,' asked Lord Abingdon in Parliament, 'does the abolition of the slave trade mean more or less in effect, than liberty and equality?'

The Abolitionists, like William Mason, Precentor of York, claimed 'that all being alike human creatures, there was neither gift nor faculty bestowed on the nature of humanity that belonged of right more to one than another of the human species'.

This claim to 'equality' that appalled Lord Abingdon still did not go far enough for Blake, as it only brought slaves to join their white brethren under the One Law. Moreover, 'equality' was not extended to the English poor, who did not share the 'same ingenuity and delicacy of mind' as the prosperous, and were 'incapable of being touched by a fine distress'.

In *Visions of the Daughters of Albion*, however, Blake not only claims liberty and equality, but denies the applicability of the oppressive universal One Law. Since the desires, aspirations, imaginations of men all differed, no law could be commonly just, and freedom was individual. And, though he may start with the idea of slavery, Blake soon brings the problem home to Lambeth, where the law of marriage iniquitously made a woman the property of her husband in a denial of human dignity, and bound a man to a life he had found loathsome. And politically, as Oothoon, the spirit of freedom, comes in from the west, Blake makes precisely the claim to 'liberty and equality' that Lord Abingdon's indignant phrase recollects. Here the poem escapes from its source, as it were, and while we have to acknowledge the initial impetus of the slavery theme, it is clear that Blake's imagination leapt at once to the analogy with Lambeth and London, where the inhabitants were slaves to prohibitions and inhibitions and expediency. Oothoon, 'the soft soul of America', personifying revolt against repressive religious and social laws, is also uninhibited and innocent love. Theotormon is desire under the severe restraint of external compulsions and its own limitations: 'And being restrained, it by degrees becomes passive, till it is only the shadow of desire.' Bromion clearly involves the false righteousness that fetters the soul, and the possessive assurance that degrades desire to self-indulgence.

Even these too simple identifications suggest how the poem transcends its own time; these issues are no less relevant to us.

The symbolism is inseparable from the theme in *Visions of the Daughters of Albion*. Indeed, the symbolism is so powerful that it generates the argument, which seems to arise out of it.

Oothoon, at the beginning of the poem, reassured that 'the

94

soul of sweet delight Can never pass away', and true marriage cannot destroy her Innocence, turns exultantly to Theotormon where her 'whole soul seeks'. At once,

> Bromion rent her with his thunders; on his stormy bed
> Lay the faint maid, and soon her woes appalled his thunders hoarse.
>
> Bromion spoke: 'Behold this harlot here on Bromion's bed,
> And let the jealous dolphins sport around the lovely maid!
> Thy soft American plains are mine, and mine thy north and south.'
>
> 16–20

—and the sons of Bromion and Oothoon will 'obey the scourge' and their granddaughters 'worship terrors and obey the violent'. Bromion is a possessive and self-perpetuating tyranny—Oothoon is 'Bromion's harlot', and protectress of his children. The poem's 'argument' begins here from the fact of the slave-owner raping his slave to increase her value; but harsh as that truth is, it remains only the beginning. There follows the deeply insidious comment upon the nature of lawful but loveless unions that prostitute marriage, and only serve the social order. 'The jealous dolphins' may also be seen initially to represent the British naval vessels; but far more important and telling is the marked change from the Innocence of Oothoon's impulsive 'swift delight' towards her lover, to the erotic image of the dolphins, with its associations with the overwhelming sea, and the sensual, possessive twist Bromion's words give to the symbol of the American plains. The initial reference in the last line is to the possession of slaves in North and South America. But that is simply the beginning.

The comments on those five lines demonstrate how the poetic symbolism carries its own meaning, and how futile (and ultimately incomprehensible) is any attempt at a kind of running explication. This simply will not work with Blake's poetry. The poem's inner illumination is either seen or missed; one can help by pointing to it, but one cannot explain it, much less paraphrase it.

Theotormon in his submission to repressive authority can only hear

> . . . like waves on a desert shore
> The voice of slaves beneath the sun, and children bought with money,
> That shiver in religious caves beneath the burning fires
> Of lust,

30–33

as he watches 'terror and meekness', Bromion and Oothoon, 'bound back to back in Bromion's caves' and folds 'his black jealous waters round the adulterate pair'. The symbolism establishes the unconventional viewpoint, made explicit when Oothoon's relationship with Bromion is called adultery. Theotormon's attitude is one of intense despair, and he is reduced to impotent inactivity while Oothoon 'hovers by his side, persuading him in vain'. The bird-like action expresses Oothoon's freedom-loving, uninhibited identity, and it is continued in a series of beautiful images of lark, nightingale, and finally the eagle, 'shaking the dust from his immortal pinions':

> Arise my Theotormon, I am pure
> Because the night is gone that closed me in its deadly black.
> They told me that the night and day were all that I could see;
> They told me that I had five senses to enclose me up,
> And they enclosed my infinite brain into a narrow circle,
> And sunk my heart into the abyss, a red, round globe, hot burning,
> Till all from life I was obliterated and erased.
> Instead of morn arises a bright shadow, like an eye
> In the eastern cloud.

51–9

We are now far beyond the initial theme of slavery, as Oothoon touches upon the genesis of Experience—the proscription of delight, and the division of eternity into a constricting sequence of days. Oothoon, in her Innocence, rejects the imposition. We now consider the philosophical basis of all human misery and degradation; Innocence and Experience are face to face.

Oothoon rejects the One Law for all creatures, for each Being is unique, 'as different as their forms and as their joys'. Innocence means complete participation in life, which Oothoon accepts, as Thel could not. Oothoon sees no sin in participation. She reiterates the unity of intellect and nature in a series of beautiful symbols, that stress the essential Innocence of interdependence:

> How can I be defiled when I reflect thy image pure?
> Sweetest the fruit that the worm feeds on, and the soul preyed on
> by woe,
> The new-washed lamb tinged with the village smoke, and the
> bright swan
> By the red earth of our immortal river.

77–80

Theotormon is helpless with self-pity, and Bromion asks the questions that lead up to the first mention of Urizen:

> And are there other sorrows beside the sorrows of poverty?
> And are there other joys beside the joys of riches and ease?
> And is there not One Law for both the lion and the ox?
> And is there not eternal fire and eternal chains
> To bind the phantoms of existence from eternal life?

106–10

The rest of the poem consists of Oothoon's furious and comprehensive indictment of Urizen, 'creator of men, mistaken demon of heaven'. 'Are not different joys Holy, eternal, infinite?' she asks, rejecting the One Law, 'and each joy is a Love.' There is nothing abstract about the challenge. She even attacks 'the fat fed hireling with hollow drum', the muster-master, 'Who buys whole corn-fields into wastes, and sings upon the heath', in contemplation of land trampled into a morass of war. We are brought to face the mystery that introduces the child in infancy to the subtlety of Experience:

97

>   . . . to catch virgin joy
> And brand it with the name of whore, and sell it in the night,
> In silence, even without a whisper, and in seeming sleep.
> Religious dreams and holy vespers light thy smoky fires.
>
> 163–6

If Theotormon seeks 'this hypocrite modesty' he is 'a sick man's dream', and Oothoon 'the crafty slave of selfish holiness'.

Oothoon's attack and her justification that 'everything that lives is holy' is varied in pace and direction. But despite the beauty of her call to love 'open to joy and delight wherever beauty appears', Theotormon's love 'drinks another as a sponge drinks water':

>   . . . self-love that envies all! a creeping skeleton
> With lamplike eyes watching around the frozen marriage bed.
>
> 196–7

The conclusion is tragic. *Visions of the Daughters of Albion* is an uncomfortable poem to read. It turns to reveal so many hypocrisies before our eyes, and today we are still afraid to acknowledge them.

v

Oothoon—the spirit of mankind that could not accept oppression and instead asserted the essential innocence of delight and desire—Oothoon was the 'soul of America'. In 1793, a few months after the appearance of *Visions*, Blake printed *America, a Prophecy*. (Of all Blake's so-called 'prophetic books' only *America* and *Europe* are given the title by the poet himself.) Here Blake gives a symbolic account of the American Revolution, and extends the strife into a conflict of prophetic range.

The 'shadowy daughter of Urthona', the 'nameless female' of the *Preludium* to *America*, occurs also in the *Preludium* to *Europe* (1794), as 'the nameless Shadowy Female'. The one develops from the other, and both are identifiable in the poetic symbolism.

In *America* she is America oppressed by Britain, under the code of Urizen. She is mankind everywhere, fallen and awaiting intellectual awakening. She is humanity, fearsomely oppressed but longing for deliverance. It is impossible to give her a single name, as her identity, in all its manifold implications, opens out in the symbolism. Moreover, the symbolism short-circuits decades, concentrating a sequence of events in a single spiralling action.

In the *Preludium* 'the shadowy daughter of Urthona' stands before 'red Orc'—the universal daughter of tyranny before the figure of revolt. Her symbolic identity is firmly established: she is shadowy, nameless, a dark virgin; she is armed for war with helmet and the bow 'like that of night' which fires the arrows of pestilence; she is 'invulnerable though naked', armed in chastity, her loins covered in clouds. She nourishes revolution, but brings the food to Orc in 'iron baskets, his drink in cups of iron'. It is her 'stern father' who has riveted the 'tenfold chains'—a chain for each perverted commandment—that hold Orc in the caverns of repression. She is as cold as frost and

> silent she stood as night;
> For never from her iron tongue could voice or sound arise,
> But dumb till that dread day when Orc assayed his fierce embrace,

in an act of coition symbolising the generation of the spirit of freedom from within the 'ancient tyranny'.

The potential revolution is universal—this is the prophecy (ll.12–17; 28–34). It will not stop at America.

It oversimplifies Blake's intentions to read Orc simply as a figure of revolt. Again, the depth and complexity of his nature are realised in the symbolism, and confirmed, as we shall see, in *Europe*. There is no Innocence in Orc. He rebels from beneath and within the dominion of Urizen. He is the 'serpent Orc', the Satanic figure of revolt from within the hierarchy. And though primarily his threat is intellectual and spiritual, his association with the symbolism of storm and lightning implies material strife. Even the command 'thou shalt not kill' has been perverted by the hierarchy in their episcopal and royal addition

—'except when our law requires it'. Blake justifies bloodshed on different grounds.

America itself extends and makes explicit the conflict set out in the *Preludium*. At the outset,

> The Guardian Prince of Albion burns in his nightly tent:
> Sullen fires across the Atlantic glow to America's shore,

the forces of monarchy and liberty are face to face, and Washington, Franklin and the other revolutionary leaders recognise the threat of force in the 'bended bow' 'lifted in heaven', and the oppressive weight of the iron chain that descends 'link by link from Albion's cliffs across the sea' to bind the Americans. Against the imagery of stars and night, from within the strife of Albion and America, Orc, the spirit of revolution, is born, from within the symbolism of oppression (ll. 19–28), and 'the King of England, looking westward, trembles at the vision'.

As in *A Song of Liberty* there is a contrast between the 'sullen flames' of Urizen, the fires that 'inwrap the earthly globe', and the 'intense, naked' 'human fire' of Orc, 'the new-born fire'. At the end of *America* this intense fire consumes the 'five gates of their law-built heaven'.

Even the dead 'spring like redeemed captives' at the resurrection of Orc, and 'the enchained soul, shut up in darkness and ·sighing' sees his 'wife and children return from the oppressor's scourge',

> For Empire is no more, and now the Lion and Wolf shall cease.

So Orc rallies the victims whose backs bear 'the furrows of the whip', recollecting the revolt of the colonies and slaves. Albion's Angel challenges Orc in the language used against the French Republicans, naming him

> Blasphemous demon, Antichrist, hater of Dignities,
> Lover of wild rebellion, and transgressor of God's Law.

56–7

So the established order is justified as divine providence, and the wider implications of the Revolution are clear in Orc's reply:

The Terror answered: 'I am Orc, wreathed round the accursed tree.
The times are ended, shadows pass, the morning 'gins to break:
The fiery joy that Urizen perverted to ten commands
What night he led the starry hosts through the wide wilderness,
That stony law I stamp to dust, and scatter religion abroad
To the four winds as a torn book, and none shall gather the leaves;
But they shall rot on desert sands and consume in bottomless deeps,
To make the deserts blossom and the deeps shrink to their fountains,
And to renew the fiery joy, and burst the stony roof.'

59–67

As the symbolism extends, the prophetic significance of the
revolt is revealed. Already the power of the eternal lion and
wolf is limited, and Albion's 'punishing demons' crouching
'before their caverns deep',

. . . cannot smite the wheat, nor quench the fatness of the earth;
They cannot smite with sorrows, nor subdue the plough and spade;
They cannot wall the city, nor moat round the castle of princes;
They cannot bring the stubbed oak to overgrow the hills.

80–3

The blight and the pestilence, the moated castle and the walled
city, are all Urizen's weapons, part of his now failing universe.
His lieutenants on earth can no longer cause the hills to be lost to
the Lamb of Innocence among 'forests of solitude'.

Orc comes against the 'aged sight' of the royalist Albion's
Angel; and the colonial forces, the Thirteen Angels, refuse 'the
loud alarm' (l. 106). They rise and revolt from inside 'the forest
of God', the submerged 'vast shady hills' beneath the Atlantic.
It is no accident that the origin of the uprising of the Thirteen
Angels recalls the location of Orc's genesis. Blake is establishing
symbolically the link between the historical act of revolt and its
prophetic implications.

Boston's Angel calls his compatriots to rebellion in a speech of
magnificent indignation. 'Must the generous tremble? . . . Who
commanded this? What God? What Angel?'

What God is he writes laws of peace and clothes him in a tempest?
What pitying Angel lusts for tears and fans himself with sighs?
What crawling villain preaches abstinence and wraps himself
In fats of lambs? No more I follow, no more obedience pay.

126–9

Though Boston's Angel carried with him the other twelve Angels, the questions he asked are still unanswered today; we still have need of the spirit of Orc.

Washington and the men of freedom are enveloped in the fires of Orc, but are inviolable. On the other hand, 'the Thirteen Governors that England sent', 'shaking their mental chains' rush into the sea, and the British soldiers throw down their muskets and desert 'their encampments and dark castles' (l. 149). The major conflict now develops. The symbolism is overwhelming. Albion's Angel opens 'his secret clouds', his 'wings of wrath' cover the eastern sky, and his camps darken the mountains, 'armed with diseases' (l. 156). The vast threatening wings recall *A Song of Liberty*, and are the counter symbol of the bird image in *Visions*.

The thunderous command of tyranny calls out the plagues from the clouds, blights the corn, and overwhelms the land:

Then had America been lost, overwhelmed by the Atlantic,
And Earth had lost another portion of the infinite.

174–5

But the plague recoils upon England, 'driven by the flames of Orc':

The doors of marriage are open, and the Priests in rustling scales
Rush into reptile coverts, hiding from the fires of Orc,
That play around the golden roofs in wreaths of fierce desire,
Leaving the females naked and glowing with the lusts of youth.

196–9

And 'they feel the nerves of youth renew', 'over their pale limbs, as a vine when the tender grape appears'. Once more Innocence triumphs, and comes through the fire which destroys the armoured sin of tyranny. Once more the poetry expands from the instant of revolt to the universal implication of that revolt, as Urizen himself intervenes with his thunder, his leprosy, his 'stored snows' and 'icy magazines':

> . . . flagged with grey-browed snows
> And thunderous visages, his jealous wings waved over the deep.
>
> 208–9

But even Urizen himself is now impotent to quench the fires of revolt.

> France, Spain and Italy
> In terror viewed the bands of Albion, and the ancient Guardians
> Fainting upon the elements, smitten with their own plagues!
> They slow advance to shut the five gates of their law-built heaven . . .

but the gates that imprison the five senses are consumed;

> . . . their bolts and hinges melted,
> And the fierce flames burnt round the heavens and round the abodes
> of men.

After a widening spiral of conflict, the triumph of Innocent desire is reiterated, and prophecy appears fulfilled. Disillusion was yet to come.

The *Preludium* to *Europe* (1794) develops the theme of the *Preludium* to *America*, where the 'shadowy daughter of Urthona' reacted to Orc's 'fierce embrace' with an intense possessiveness: 'I know thee, I have found thee, and I will not let thee go.'
In the opening lines of the *Preludium* to *Europe* we learn that:

> The nameless Shadowy Female rose from the breast of Orc
> Her snaky hair brandishing in the winds of Enitharmon.

Once again, it is impossible and undesirable to identify the mythological characters exactly.
In *Europe* Blake begins with the aftermath of the American War of Independence, and goes on to give an apocalyptic significance to the war in north-east France and the Netherlands

in 1794. Here, in King George's own words, the Duke of York was making 'the greatest exertion to attempt to save Europe and society itself'. But the French were now reorganised by Carnot, and they drove the Duke back across the Meuse, and forced his recall to England.

Blake does not relate these events directly. Indeed, it was hardly possible for him to do this, as his notion of the salvation of Europe and society was the reverse of his King's. So a symbolism here more cryptic and difficult than in *America* conceals the historical events, but at the same time enables Blake to relate his theme to conditions in London, and to give the Republican advance a significance against a time-scale of eighteen hundred years. So the language of the poem is carrying a formidable weight of meaning, and, despite the heady promise for revolutionaries of 1794, is loaded with tragic reservations.

We may see the 'nameless Shadowy Female' as Humanity that at once welcomes and perverts the fires of truth. She may be nature; she may be the female principle that dominates under Urizen (even subverting his power) through sexual possession. In the first two lines of the *Preludium*, she rises from the fiery breast of Orc, not redeemed and purified, but garlanded in sin, and bewailing the possibility that her dominion might end. At a political level, as Humanity she needs and cries for the redeeming freedom of Orc, and yet, as a human being, she is afraid at the loss of status and degree her wish implies.

Enitharmon, as the mother of the 'nameless Shadowy Female', shapes and dictates the precepts by which mankind is gently ensnared, and she seeks to control inspiration, stamping it 'with a signet'. And, as always in Blake, the poem demands that we draw a parallel between political-revolutionary themes and the simple case of men and women bound in the 'chartered streets' of London, and nourishing their jealousies behind the garden walls of Lambeth. *Europe* tells no simple story in terms of myth and symbol, and we cannot fix the mythological relationship in a kind of genealogical tree. The reader who looks for a narrative will close the book in frustration. Blake asks the reader to let his imagination quicken, as it were at the axle of a wheel of time and space, while his vision radiates to the circumference, without questioning closely the rational limitations. The vision may be powerful at times, or obscure. If it is rarely clear, it is never obvious. In all this, it may reflect the inexpressible motives of humanity and inhumanity more closely than we like.

The 'nameless Shadowy Female' is already dominated by Enitharmon. She is forced to self-effacement and secrecy (l. 5), and subject to a thunderous tyranny; she is compelled to constant travail in sin, and yet must contemplate the celestial hosts, and from this heavenly reckoning (l. 16) she brings forth 'all devouring, fiery kings',

> Devouring and devoured, roaming on dark and desolate mountains,
> In forests of Eternal Death.

20–1

So the dilemma and tragedy of mankind is put to us. Sin labours to deliver tyranny; the appalled and forced contemplation of the Divine brings us among 'the forests of Eternal Death'. At the same time, humanity is often truly inspired, and brings forth 'myriads of flames'; at once such revolutionary ideas are censured, controlled, stamped 'with a signet' of official approval, and humanity that aspired to Orc-like liberty is left 'drowned in shady woe and visionary joy'—a ghostly fulfilment (ll. 24–7).

The last stanza of the *Preludium* establishes the visionary relationship between Orc and the true Christ:

> And who shall bind the Infinite with an eternal band
> To compass it with swaddling bands? and who shall cherish it
> With milk and honey?
> I see it smile and roll inward and my voice is past.

28–31

Infinite perception, infinite charity, infinite joy—all this has already been swaddled and cherished with soft delusions, and the 'milk and honey' of tenderness in the person of Christ the infant, till the terrible challenge of His true teaching has been drawn, and humanity left with inward contemplation and illusion.

The *Preludium* takes us to this point, where the *Prophecy* itself begins. In the dreamful peace following the 'swaddling' of the young spirit of revolt,

> War ceased, and all the troops like shadows fled to their abodes.

In the person of Los, mankind takes solace 'in the peaceful night', and, the true Christ being kept 'secret', Urizen is 'unloosed from chains' and 'glows like a meteor'. The sons of Urizen envy the delights of Los, and seek to share his peaceful indulgence. The imagery recollects the Vale of Har:

> Seize all the spirits of life and bind
> Their warbling joys to our loud strings!
> Bind all the nourishing sweets of earth
> To give us bliss, that we may drink the sparkling wine of Los!
> And let us laugh at war,
> Despising toil and care,
> Because the days and nights of joy in lucky hours renew.
>
> 17–23

Orc is bound, and may therefore be honoured with garlands. Lip-service to spiritual regeneration is enough, while the delights of effeminate moonlight make a pleasant mockery of true peace. At this stage, the fire of rebellion is fading in lassitude. We have not yet reached the French victories of 1794, and on the vaster time-scale Enitharmon's address to her children (one of whom is Orc, now bound, and another the Shadowy Female) echoes back from the heavens:

> Now comes the night of Enitharmon's joy!
> Who shall I call? Who shall I send,
> That woman, lovely woman may have dominion?
> Arise O Rintrah, thee I call, and Palamabron thee!
> Go, tell the human race that woman's love is sin,
> That an eternal life awaits the worms of sixty winters,
> In an allegorical abode where existence hath never come.

Forbid all joy; and from her childhood shall the little female
Spread nets in every secret path.

33-42

Rintrah is to bring Palamabron, who is 'the horned priest
skipping upon the mountains' (l. 47), and is coupled here with
the queen of silence and moonlight (l. 46). Rintrah's bride weeps
and is jealous, hidden by him 'in desert shades' (l. 48). Rintrah is
supreme among these lieutenants. While Palamabron is the priest
associated with the aloof and cynical 'chastity' of the silver
mountain tops and moonlight, Rintrah, the proud lion of royal
lust on earth, arises from his 'forests black'. The symbolism of
seductive repression becomes formidable indeed when Blake
adds to it the royal power of Rintrah, nurtured in the forests of
affliction that have overwhelmed the hills of Innocence—
Rintrah the 'King of Fire', 'Prince of the Sun', whose 'innumer-
able race, Thick as the summer stars', shake their golden manes.
He is 'second to none but Orc'.

So powerful is the fascination of Enitharmon that the dreamful
sleep lasts from the Nativity to the Revolution—

Eighteen hundred years: Man was a dream!
The night of Nature and their harps unstrung!

56-7

Line 60 begins another chapter in the poem. Blake takes no
account of time sequence in *Europe*, and here he moves from a
glance at the defeat of Albion's Angels at the hands of the
American revolutionaries, to a preview of the infinite theme of
creation and repression he develops fully in *The Book of Urizen*.
Put lamely, he may be saying that tyranny, faced with defeat,
retreats to its 'oak surrounded pillars, formed of massy stones'
(l. 77), and falls back on the old eternal verities, established
when

Thought changed the Infinite to a serpent, that which pitieth
To a devouring flame; and man fled from its face and hid
In forests of night. Then all the eternal forests were divided
Into earths, rolling in circles of Space, that like an ocean rushed
And overwhelmed all except this finite wall of flesh.

107

> Then was the Serpent temple formed, image of Infinite,
> Shut up in finite revolutions, and Man became an angel,
> Heaven a mighty circle turning, God a tyrant crowned.
>
> 86–93

The symbolism is the only means of transition from the immediate historic conflict to the cosmic event, and it is the only way Blake can relate the two. It is not a question of cause and effect, from concept to historical consequence. War generates evil, evil generates war—cause and effect are lost in a vicious circle. In *Europe* the circle turns around us.

The 'Ancient Guardian' flees to his temple, ominously 'o'er-hung with purple flowers and berries red' (l. 97), and the temple exists in the mind, beneath the 'stony roof' (l. 99) of the human skull. The retreat is made to ancient intellectual ramparts.

In *America* mankind came unscathed through the fire, provided the precept was observed that 'everything that lives is holy', and at the end of *America* the five senses, the five gates of the 'law-built Heaven', were 'unable to stem the fires of Orc', being filled with 'blasting fancies', 'fierce disease and lust'. Now again Orc's fires attack the flesh of Albion's Angel, clouded by Rintrah and the phantasies of Enitharmon. Just as the poem revolved to infinite and metaphysical range from a hint of the American revolution, so now (ll. 102 et seq.) the whole vast abstract oppression of Urizen concentrates on London, until the fires of Orc consume the flesh of 'Aged Ignorance', and the 'Guardian of the secret codes' is 'driven out by the flames of Orc'.

But the rejoicings of Orc are brought to an end by the legionary might of King and priest (ll. 129–30), and immediately

> Enitharmon laughed in her sleep to see (O woman's triumph!)
> Every house a den, every man bound. The shadows are filled
> With spectres, and the windows wove over with curses of iron:
> Over the doors, 'Thou shalt not,' and over the chimneys 'Fear' is
> written.
>
> 131–4

The 'mighty spirit' who finally succeeds in blowing the 'trump of the last doom' is Newton. In other terms, the mechanistic universe, derived from Newton's thinking, made of infinity 'a mighty circle turning', ordered the stars, and turned the skies into mills controlled by Urizen and Enitharmon. The quasi-Newtonian thinking of the 18th century was seen by Blake as part of the enormous confidence trick perpetuating oppression.

The sound rouses Enitharmon. Her adult, sensual, self-conscious delight is evident in her song, fashioned in familiar imagery (ll. 157–91), and she attempts the seduction of Orc among her 'dreamful caves' and mountains:

> But terrible Orc, when he beheld the morning in the East,
> Shot from the heights of Enitharmon,
> And in the vineyards of red France appeared the light of his fury.
>
> 197–9

The dream of Enitharmon is mangled in the revolution of 'red wheels dropping with blood'. The pleasures of Los are dispelled now that Orc is unbound. The universal conflict is unresolved, indeed hardly begun, and in the end:

> Los arose; his head he reared, in snaky thunders clad,
> And with a cry that shook all Nature to the utmost pole,
> Called all his sons to the strife of blood.

This tough, intransigent poem is quite without solace. Critics have used such phrases as 'the persistence of Blake's hope and even enthusiasm in 1794' when writing of *Europe*. I can see none of this, only pity, terror, illusion, the inevitable commitment either to battle or brute submission, and the eternal victims bred in the generations across eighteen hundred years. If Blake knew hope and enthusiasm, he knew them stalked by tragedy. As inheritors of half a century of war, we at least should understand him.

7

Urizen and Experience

The basic 'story' of *The Book of Urizen* (1794) is as old and familiar as hymn singing. Isaac Watts in *God's Dominions and Decrees*, for instance:

> The Almighty Voice bid ancient night
>   Her endless realms resign,
> And lo, ten thousand globes of light
>   In fields of azure shine.
>
> Now Wisdom with superior sway
>   Guides the vast moving frame,
> Whilst all the ranks of being pay
>   Deep reverence to His name.
>
> Lord of the armies of the sky
>   He marshals all the stars.
> Red comets lift their banners high
>   And wide proclaim His wars.
>
> Chained to His throne a volume lies
>   With all the fates of men,
> With every angel's form and size
>   Drawn by the eternal pen.

It is easy for us to accept that account of the creation and ordering of the universe, because we have been so well trained to accept it.

Here in 1709 Isaac Watts shows proper respect to the god Blake later called Urizen. It is a servitude which sickened the poet. Yet how easily we share it.

The challenge of *Urizen* lies in the fact that Blake discredits and condemns this old and perhaps not yet out-worn dispensation. It is not long since the Almighty was both judge and executioner at the beck and call of men established in power; the law of God was made to reflect the law of the state, and still may be. It is no simple coincidence that the real understanding of Blake's poetry is an achievement of the last twenty-five years or so, when old concepts of the nature of God have been questioned. If we stand back a moment from our preconceptions, and read that poem by Watts *through Blake's eyes*, it becomes almost a summary of *Urizen*. The Almighty separates creation from eternity, he fixes the stars in their inevitable and predetermined courses, he requires homage from beings divided into ranks, he feeds on war, the stars of night serve his ancient armies, he determines man's fate, making the rich prosperous and the poor impoverished, he keeps the account, and he is royalty incarnate. This, indeed, is Urizen. Watts tells the same story as Blake, without the tragic condemnation.

When we sing the many hymns written more or less in the manner of Isaac Watts, we do so unthinkingly. If asked, few people today would accept the secret, watchful, aloof adjudicator as a Divine Idea. But we still find *The Book of Urizen* making intense demands on our imagination, because it remains a unique and comprehensive denial of a principle that has dominated mankind down the generations—the Creator with a seat on the King's Bench, and the God of Love as a dispenser of licensed philanthropy.

All great literature illuminates its own age and throws a light towards posterity. In *Urizen* Blake is free from the exercise of concealment that the political themes imposed on him in the other Prophetic Books. Here Blake deals with the philosophical assumptions that pretend to virtue, and breed evil under furred gowns. There are no direct political references, and the critics who relate Blake's writing to historical events have little to say on *Urizen*. None the less, the simple release from the fear of the censor means that Blake is released from the inhibitions of his age. In consequence he speaks to us more directly; and *Urizen* is the climax of the shorter Prophetic Books.

In *The Book of Urizen* Blake deals with the original division of infinity and eternity into space and time, and the creation of the world and mankind. The central conflict of the poem lies in the paradox that Urizen is identified as both creator and oppressor. The initial act of creation itself arises from the separation of Urizen from eternal life, just as on earth the teaching of Urizen, while laying claim to divine authority, obliterates the eternal parts of man. Urizen is at once a god and the organised perversion of the idea of God.

Urizen's act of creation brings chaos to the flowing order of eternity. The chaos is then contained within finite limits. For Blake, anything fixed and changeless implied death of body and and soul. The mechanistic universe, the unalterable One Law, the sustained tyranny of political institutions, the preservation of social order based on injustice, the imagination restricted by aesthetic conventions, inspiration confined by censorship, the fostering of children to the acceptance of a preconceived dogma —all these were aspects of a common oppression, physical, intellectual and spiritual. The effect was universal, and in *The Book of Urizen* Blake gives it an inescapable genesis in the Creation itself.

Simultaneously with this creation, mankind is imprisoned in his five senses, and confined to mortality and an existence of spiritual loneliness:

> This Urizen perceived, and silent brooded in darkening clouds.
> To him his labour was but sorrow, and his kingdom repentance.
>
> THE FOUR ZOAS XI

A consequence of Urizen's acts is the separation of mankind from his brethren in other cities, the web of religion, the disease of jealousy and cruelty—indeed the universe of Experience. *Urizen* is an account of the creation of the form of life upon which *Songs of Experience* offer specific commentaries. All the evils of Experience feed upon the dogma of absolute reaction to change.

Blake was not the first poet to attempt an account of the Creation in terms of a facile and popular conception of the mechanistic universe based on Newton's physics. Indeed, the Creation had long been related to 'laws of prudence', and Blake's own central paradox of Creation had been wanly anticipated by Sir Richard Blackmore in his *Creation: A Philosophical Poem* (1712):

> Could chance such just and prudent measures take?
> To frame the world such *distribution* make?

And Blackmore's respectable progenitor of Urizen had already set his compasses in the infinite, and fixed the 'starry roof'—precisely the idea Blake sees as enclosing mankind against infinity:

> Did this your wise and sovereign architect
> Design the model and the world erect,
> Were by his skill the deep foundations laid,
> The globes suspended and the heavens displayed?
> By what elastic engines did he rear
> The starry roof and roll the orbs in air?

The cosmic measuring, the dividing, the philosophical systematisation are all there. By 1796 many pupils who read *The Study of Astronomy, adapted to the capacities of Youth*, by John Stedman, had 'heard of the *numbering* of the stars', and how the ancients had *reduced* astronomy to a science for 'the better distinguishing of things'. We should not today speak of creation in terms of 'numbering' the stars; yet this, with the idea of earth 'receiving her *frame*', was commonplace in Blake's day. The idea of 'setting a bound' upon the infinite is clearly evident in this way of thinking. The analogy between this 'astronomy' and social order is easy to see.

In Blackmore and others there is approval that leads inevitably to a facile reassurance. When James Thomson 'in some deep retirement'

> would search if nature's boundless frame
> Was called, late-rising, from the void of night,
> Or sprung eternal from the Eternal Mind,

WINTER, 575–8

he would then

> try to scan the moral world,
> Which, though to us it seems embroiled, moves on
> In highest order, fitted and impelled
> By wisdom's finest hand, and issuing all
> In general good.

WINTER, 583–7

It is as if the mechanistic universe simply demonstrated the ordered nature of the Creator's purposes—ordered to meet and further 'the general good' of society as it stood. Preachers, like Augustus Toplady, could refer to 'Our God in his heavens', sitting 'upon his throne, weighing out and dispensing the fates of men . . . guiding every link of the chain of second courses, from the beginning to the end of time', and then with an appropriate glance at the mechanistic universe, warn men not 'to clog the wheels of divine government'.

Here is Urizen among his 'starry wheels'. But Toplady approves. And in both the sermons and the poetry, science and religion enjoy a mutual confirmation that is thoroughly acceptable. But whereas Blackmore writes apparently 'scientific' verse, he is dull because he raises no questions and starts no alarms. In *Urizen* Blake reacts not only to the religious but also to the scientific platitudes of his age. His imagination cannot accept the validity of a universe of interacting wheels. Or rather, he sees this as simply another manifestation of Urizen's tyrannous deception.

So *Urizen* is written round a theme that recurs in hymns, sermons and pseudo-epic poetry. There is nothing odd about *Urizen*; it is simply unique in its line of vision. And the critical difficulty for the reader lies in the initial acceptance of this uniqueness. Nowhere else is symbolism used with such assurance to deal at length with a theme and conflict of this magnitude.

The first chapter of *Urizen* gives us an introductory summary. Urizen is generated in abstraction; he is a creature of no substance, 'a shadow of horror', 'unknown, unprolific, self-closed, all-repelling'. He is secret and brooding. He creates an 'abominable void, This soul-shuddering vacuum' out of the living flux of eternity, then, out of this chaos, a universe and earthly life fastened within finite sensibility.

> Times on times he divided and measured,
> Space by space in his ninefold darkness,

> I, 2

until the elements and creatures that inhabit them are 'bred from his forsaken wilderness'. Even in the act of creation, Urizen is engaged in secret enmity with the creatures that evolve. He detests the issue of his own barrenness.

With a glance at the wheeling universe, Blake describes Urizen as 'Dark, revolving in silent activity', and associates this symbol of mill and wheel with the negative self-contemplation of Urizen, put to us most forcibly in forest and sea symbolism already familiar:

> But Eternals beheld his vast forests;
> Ages on ages he lay, closed, unknown,
> Brooding shut in the deep. All a void
> The petrific, abominable chaos.

> I, 5

After the summary in Chapter 1, Blake returns to the genesis of things before the coming of Urizen's petrific chaos, when

> Earth was not, nor globes of attraction;
> The will of the Immortal expanded
> Or contracted his all-flexible senses;
> Death was not, but eternal life sprung.

> II, 1

Urizen cannot tolerate the ever-changing life of the Eternals, which is akin to Innocence. So in *The Four Zoas*, XI, Blake tells how, in Innocence once, Los and Enitharmon

<blockquote>
walked forth on the dewy earth
Contracting and expanding their all-flexible senses,
At will to murmur in the flowers small as the honey bee,
At will to stretch across the heavens and step from star to star.
</blockquote>

This quality cannot be 'determined by measure', nor seen with the natural eye. It belongs to 'the eye of the imagination', which creatively transmutes what it sees to spiritual significance. So Urizen, seeking changelessness, creates his rock of Albion, and writes 'the secrets of dark contemplation' (II, 6) in his 'book of eternal brass', 'petrifying all the human imagination into rock and sand', and offering specious 'laws of peace, of love, of unity'. Then

<blockquote>
Let each choose one habitation,
His ancient infinite mansion,
One command, one joy, one desire,
One curse, one weight, one measure,
One King, one God, one Law.
</blockquote>

II, 8

The promise of infinity under a roof, and the inevitable changeless law, are the beginning of Experience. Soon 'all the seven deadly sins of the soul' are breathed into every bosom. Urizen with his 'self-begotten armies' piles up 'mountains and hills' 'in incessant labour' to avoid the 'flames of eternal fury', till he fades

<blockquote>
age-broke, and aged
In despair and the shadows of death.
</blockquote>

III, 6

Urizen has turned into the Ancient Father of men—'Old Nobodaddy' Blake called him. The 'vast world of Urizen' appears 'like a human heart'. Urizen is 'laid in strong sleep', and 'rent from eternity' (III, 10).

Los, in this book a figure of titanic range, 'affrighted at the formless, unmeasurable death' that derives from Urizen 'rent from eternity', rouses his fires to bind 'the dark changes' of

Urizen—'every change With rivets of iron and brass'. But first he divides eternity into time, 'the horrible night into watches', as Urizen 'divided and measured' infinity into space. Then Los forges mankind out of the changes of Urizen, motivated not by the desire to create, but in fear of death. In

> Forgetfulness, dumbness, necessity,
> In chains of the mind locked up,
> Like fetters of ice shrinking together,

IVB, 4

—a passage of terrifying insistence—the body of mankind is forged round 'Urizen, deadly, black':

> And now his Eternal Life,
> Like a dream, was obliterated.

V, 3

But the horror of the sight of Urizen embodied in mankind transfixes Los, 'the eternal prophet':

> The bellows and hammer are silent now,
> A nerveless silence his prophetic voice
> Seized; a cold solitude and dark void,
> The Eternal Prophet and Urizen closed.

V, 4

The inspiration of Los is frozen into deformity while his fires decay, and he is absorbed into Urizen, whose influence becomes universal. The tragedy lies here, in that all moves to contain the oppressive tyranny seem only to feed it. Urizen is forged into man's frame, and the Eternal Prophet, afraid of eternity, looks back at his ancient eternal life

> with anxious desire,
> But the space, undivided by existence,
> Struck horror into his soul.

V, 5

Urizen has reduced the immortal vision to a nervous fear. Pity now 'divides the soul', and Woman, Enitharmon, is born, among 'curtains of darkness'. And

Eternity shuddered when they saw
Man begetting his likeness
On his own Divided Image.

VI, 2

Enitharmon gives birth to Orc, who is at once chained

> to the rock
> With the chain of jealousy
> Beneath Urizen's deathful shadow,

VII, 4

Urizen roams his dens, and sickens to see his world and its enormities.

Now we witness the rank dissemination of Urizen's influence over Creation. The inspiration of Los is inhibited and curtained in effeminacy. Orc is chained. The sons of Urizen are born of the barren rock, the sand, and the waters of material creation; his daughters of the flesh and the plant. Imagination brings forth no offspring. And we come to the universal law of iron, promulgated by Urizen from his dark abode, though

> no flesh nor spirit could keep
> His iron laws one moment.

VIII, 4

Urizen is aware of this; and the reason for his awareness is death:

> For he saw that life lived upon death:
> The ox in the slaughter-house moans,
> The dog at the wintry door.
> And he wept and he called it Pity,
> And his tears flowed down on the winds.

VIII, 5

The pity of Urizen is a lament at his own Creation; it is self-pity, and the pity of the feral beast 'stung with the odours of nature'. Wherever Urizen wanders, a 'cold shadow' follows him,

Drawing out from his sorrowing soul,
The dungeon-like heaven dividing.

VIII, 6

Among mankind, Urizen walks 'over the cities in sorrow',

Till a web, dark and cold, throughout all
The tormented element stretched
From the sorrows of Urizen's soul;

VIII, 7

—a web which 'no wings of fire' can break, which is 'twisted like to the human brain', and which is simultaneously the curtain of effeminacy and 'the net of religion'. Beneath Urizen's 'dark net of infection' the inhabitants of the cities

Felt their nerves change into marrow
And hardening bones began
In swift diseases and torment,

IX, 1

death being the direct consequence of Urizen's dominance; death not only of the body, but of the perceptions during mortal life. Divided, and roofed within cities, the people forget 'their eternal life', and 'shrink together Beneath the net of Urizen'. And instead of Innocent participation

their children wept, and built
Tombs in the desolate places,
And formed laws of prudence and called them
The eternal laws of God.

IX, 5

The division and the enslavement are complete. The cities of Urizen's creation remain 'surrounded by salt floods', and the inhabitants live in perpetual separation from brotherhood:

And their eyes could not discern
Their brethren of other cities.

IX, 7

Urizen has created the realms of Experience not only on earth, but in the human brain.

In 1793 Blake had moved to 13 Hercules Buildings, in Lambeth, just across Westminster Bridge. From Lambeth he launched his attack upon the whole political, moral, philosophical and psychological set-up that created 'the terrible desert of London' over the river. The three years following the move were the most creative in Blake's life. Above all, in 1794 he added *Songs of Experience* to *Songs of Innocence*, to make up one of the supremely great volumes of short poems in the language—and the event was scarcely noticed.

Along the Lambeth river front, in Prince's Meadows (leased from the Prince Regent), were twenty-nine acres of dye-houses, storehouses, accounting houses, brew-houses, stables, coach-houses, saw-houses, cranes, wharves, ponds, gardens, canals, and seventy dwelling houses. Above all stood the square shot tower, in 1791 described as 'a new structure . . . [which] cannot be considered as an object ornamental to the River Thames'. Near Blake's house was the Asylum for Female Orphans opened 'in a house lately the Hercules Inn near Westminster Bridge', by a group of 'noblemen and gentlemen' for girls between nine and twelve years old, 'to save them from the guilt of prostitution', and even from their own destitute mothers who have 'for some trifling consideration' 'ensnared their children to the house of the procuress'. As Blake put it, 'beauty for a bit of bread'.

Opposite the Asylum, which at once salved the social con-science and supplied society with domestic servants trained in pious and grateful discipline, stood the Apollo Gardens, disreput-able now, in a tired way, and run by one Crispus Claggett. It was Crispus who rebuilt the Pantheon in 1794, prefabricating the timbered roof in a field near his Gardens and carting it over Westminster Bridge. He vanished unaccountably in 1796 and was discovered as a skeleton forty years later under his own stage.

Another showman, Philip Astley, had taken 'a large piece of ground, of a timber merchant, near Westminster Bridge, on the Surrey side', and by 1783 this 'riding master for the Royal Grove and Amphitheatre' was licensed to present stage performances. A year after Blake arrived in Lambeth his theatre (by then the Royal Saloon) was burnt down—another spectacular fire. But Astley continued to live in Hercules Hall, at the back of Blake's house, and they came near to blows when Blake discovered a boy chained by Astley to a log 'in a way inexcusable even towards a slave'. But the shackling of children by employers and in the factories was commonplace.

Within a few minutes' walk of Blake's house was Newington Butts, where the rectory was 'a very ancient wooden building, surrounded by a moat, over which are four bridges'. This rectory brings together strangely the ideas of the castle and war, the separate aloofness, and the orthodox worship associated by Blake with the 'rotten wood' of which Tiriel was king.

Up river from Hercules Hall, a decent distance beyond Lambeth Palace, were the famous and extensive Vauxhall Gardens, much more fashionable and more elegantly disreputable than Crispus Claggett's place. Vauxhall Gardens were 'the most celebrated' in Europe, with a principal walk 'terminated by a transparency, emblematic of gratitude for public patronage', Ionic columns, statues, and the inscription, beside a painting of General Amherst at the conquest of Montreal:

Power Executed, Conquest Obtained, Mercy Shown 1760

Here also was 'Britannia, holding in her hand a medallion of his present majesty, and sitting on the right hand of Neptune in his chariot drawn by sea horses'.

This is precisely the power, conquest and mercy Blake attacked in the Lambeth Books, and this Neptune shares his ocean with Britannia in the name of commerce and slavery.

The Lambeth where Blake lived epitomised in a fascinating way the abstract thinking that perpetuated the misery of London. And supreme, of course, among all the organised improvement south of the river was Lambeth Palace, the home of the Archbishop. The gardens of Hercules Buildings and of the new Bond Estate built in the fields to the south lead easily into the gardens of Experience, where each man nursed his jealous desires among the symbolic myrtles and rose trees. And, indeed, in 1793, a group of property developers built the South Lambeth Chapel (now rebuilt as St. Anne's Church) to serve this prosperous estate. They might well have consecrated it outright to Urizen. It was a proprietary chapel, the cost of building being covered by an issue of sixty £50 shares. Each shareholder was entitled to four seats. The rest of the congregation of six hundred all had to be approved by the proprietors and able to pay a rent for their seats, none being free. The Rector of St. Mary's, Lambeth, nominated the minister, and the proprietors paid his salary. Listen to the priest of Urizen preaching in Lambeth among the gardens of Experience, reassuring this licensed congregation of the advantage of poverty they lack:

> If the poor envy the rich, as exempt from that drudgery to which they are subject, the rich may sometimes, with more justice, envy the industrious and temperate poor; because that very drudgery prevents that idle swarm of restless thoughts that . . . inaction sometimes breeds in them. The labour of the body . . . procures them peace of mind . . . They bid as fair for a competency as the rich themselves, if not fairer. For their labour, to which they are constantly inured, takes up their thoughts, and hinders them from straggling abroad.

The jealousy, the heart-sickness, the 'restless thoughts' that weave so tragically through *Songs of Experience* are not solely Blake's personal reactions to private emotions. They slip too easily into the Lambeth landscape for that. In the gardens of Experience we see growing the fears and false desires, the melancholy sexual solace of Urizen's prosperity—a solace that the poor ('industrious and temperate' or not) had neither privacy nor time for. In the voice of the proprietors' priest we hear Urizen reassuring the inhabitants of the gardens.

So again the symbolism of *Songs of Experience* derives from a contemporary situation. The Songs direct our imagination to the desolation of soul which invades the leisured and righteous prosperity that society fosters with such propriety. And once again, these most uncomfortable poems even today illuminate our own delicately curtained desires.

iv

Blake was intensely and mystically attached to his younger brother, Robert, who had died in 1787; so much so that even in 1800 Blake related how he would converse with Robert 'daily and hourly in the spirit, and see him in my remembrance, in the regions of my imagination'. Blake also possessed a notebook (now known as Blake's *Notebook*, or the *Rossetti MS*, after D. G. Rossetti who once owned it) which he treasured as it had belonged to Robert, and in which *Songs of Experience* and related poems were first written. So precious were the pages that Blake covered every inch of their surface with sketches and poems, even overwriting the drawings with corrections of the poems.

All the poems Blake wrote in the *Notebook* are tense, concentrated, and disillusioned at the prospect of hypocrisy triumphant in youth and age. As in *Never seek to tell thy love*, the promiscuous invasions of Experience always succeed, with sorrow as an inevitable consequence; and the cynical advice against the frankness of Innocence in that poem is the basis for bringing up children in *A Cradle Song*, Blake's first attempt at writing a 'contrary' to a Song of Innocence. Here the secrecy of Urizen and the enticements of Enitharmon are bred into the infant in the cradle, and the 'dreadful lightnings' break from this to blight the harvest of his youth. The parent's touch upon the child is sensually expectant:

> Sweet babe, in thy face
> Soft desires I can trace,
> Secret joys and secret smiles,
> Little pretty infant wiles.
>
> As thy softest limbs I feel,
> Smiles as of the morning steal
> O'er thy cheek and o'er thy breast
> Where the little heart does rest.

A CRADLE SONG

123

The 'morning' here is the dawn of Experience, the illusory counter-image to the sunrise of Innocence.

Mary Wollstonecraft (the mother of Mary Shelley) had written that 'children are taught revenge and lies in their very cradles', and 'strange prejudices and vain fears' bred into their minds. She protested that children 'would play harmlessly together, if the distinction of sex was not inculcated long before nature makes any difference'.

It was an education that served an adult and experienced purpose. The purpose was to reconcile an acceptable morality and an erotic necessity. We may see this reflected in James Thomson's description of the Daughters of Britannia. In her enticements, and of course her power, such a daughter could be Blake's Enitharmon; she is at once chaste, suffused with religious awe, sensual and aloof—

> The neck slight-shaded and the swelling breast;
> The look resistless, piercing to the soul,
> And by the soul informed, when dressed in love
> She sits high-smiling in the conscious eye.

SUMMER, 1590-3

The chastity 'inculcated' in youth was self-consciously absorbed, and developed in a way Blake related to Experience:

> . . . clear Chastity,
> With blushes reddening as she moves along,
> Disordered at the deep regard she draws.

1609-11

Blake knew Mary Wollstonecraft and her views well, and he turned the reformer's advanced thinking into poetry in which we recognise our own adult anticipation, which caresses the infant inevitably towards Experience. The points made by Mary Wollstonecraft (and any other reformer) concern other people's blindness, and we are satisfied to agree, and be exonerated. Blake does not make us feel so comfortably enlightened. He commits us to our own imaginations.

When Blake writes in the first person, the 'I' hardly ever means exclusively Blake himself. For all his intense commitment, he is much more capable of depersonalising his feelings than other Romantic poets. By transferring a conflict, either personal or social, into symbolism he dissociates his private feelings. In a way, though of course a different way, this is what a dramatist does. And Blake has something of what Keats called Shakespeare's 'negative capability'. When Wordsworth writes of daffodils, or Keats writes about a nightingale, we are aware all along of the poet's presence. This egocentric quality, the subjective direction of the thought, is said to typify Romantic poetry. If Blake is a Romantic poet, the generalisation is worthless. We are rarely conscious of Blake as a person in his poems; he almost invariably achieves an objective realisation of his emotions in a symbolic action.

In *A Cradle Song* no one would claim that 'I' meant Blake himself. It may not be very different even in *My Pretty Rose-tree*:

A flower was offered to me,
Such a flower as May never bore;
But I said, 'I've a pretty rose-tree,'
And I passed the sweet flower o'er.

Then I went to my pretty rose-tree,
To tend her by day and by night;
But my rose turned away with jealousy,
And her thorns were my only delight.

This Song of Experience is the first poem in the *Notebook*, and the identity behind the flower that, May never bore' has been seen as Mary Wollstonecraft herself. The 'rose-tree', the symbol of love under Urizen, is always tended with jealousy in the garden of Experience, and here is taken to represent Catherine Blake. So the poem is a symbolic presentation of some extra-marital incident, in, say, 1792, with Catherine apparently unappreciative of William's candour. This is about as near as we get to a strictly autobiographical poem in Blake.

Now even here, the actual incident and the identities are

unimportant. The 'flower' may be Mary Wollstonecraft (aged thirty-three); but it may be (though nobody gives her the credit) Elizabeth Billington, the incomparable *prima donna*, then twenty-six, who lived a few doors from Blake at 54 Poland Street and was known as 'the Poland Street man-trap', because of her accommodating temperament.

The point is how little it matters, even in a poem most likely to be based on an intimately personal incident. The experience is generalised in the symbolism.

On the other hand, it is important that places like the proprietary chapel in the South Lambeth fields were being built when Blake wrote *The Garden of Love*, beginning:

> I went to the Garden of Love,
> And saw what I never had seen:
> A chapel was built in the midst
> Where I used to play on the green.

Like all *Songs of Innocence and of Experience* the poem communicates its meaning to us even if we are ignorant of Blake's London. But if we know that in Blake's day the greens round which a communal life was centred were being appropriated by builders of estates served with such chapels, the poem takes on an added dimension from history. Moreover it is relevant, because we are the inheritors and victims of the process Blake exposed and condemned. This knowledge is critically relevant, in a way that the hypothesis of a personal affair concerning Blake himself is not, because in the personal case the poet's whole intention is to exclude himself and to involve us in a recognised experience.

In *Songs of Experience* Blake traces the footsteps of Urizen into the bedrooms and nurseries of London and through the gardens of Lambeth. He exposes the secret conflict that lies at the heart of the most intimate thought, and the symbolism and directness transmute the bitterness into tragedy. It was a true 'Augury of Innocence',

> To see a World in a grain of sand
> And Heaven in a wild flower,

but in Experience, Urizen, 'dark, revolving in silent activity, Unseen', lodges his disease and death in the flower of love:

O Rose, thou art sick!
The invisible worm
That flies in the night,
In the howling storm,

Has found out thy bed
Of crimson joy,
And his dark secret love
Does thy life destroy.

The symbolism there gives range and general relevance to a profound personal despair. But any autobiographical guesswork is intrusive, since the poet has unsaid his personal sentiments in settling the evil on Everyman. Blake is symbolising the concealed corrosion of the 'immoral' marriage law that established and perpetuated loveless relationships, often making virtues of expediency and possessiveness. The 'invisible worm', the germ of moral disease, is given an intelligence allied in its self-seeking destructiveness to that of the traveller in *Never seek to tell thy love* who moved 'silently, invisibly' on the winds of seduction. But the seduction belongs to Urizen for encouragement. All the viewpoints of *The Sick Rose* are directed to the physical aspects of life and death, yet against this the invisible nature of the corruption speaks for its spiritual genesis. The vision contracts inward. The symbolic identity between the flower and the grace of love remains valid; but the symbol no longer expands to infinity. Instead the storm buries itself in the bloom. This is no 'wild flower', but a rose fostered in the gardens of Experience, in the knowledge 'that woman's love is sin'.

If the imagination does turn away from the earth in *Songs of Experience*, it is not towards eternity, but towards 'an allegorical abode where existence hath never come', towards 'the lost traveller's dream under the hill'. The imagination is confined to following the sun each day in a series of tedious revolutions. The Sunflower, 'weary of time', seeks inspiration in vain, and divides eternity into days measuring out her release:

Ah, Sunflower, weary of time,
Who countest the steps of the sun,
Seeking after that sweet golden clime
Where the traveller's journey is done;

Where the youth pined away with desire,
And the pale virgin shrouded in snow,
Arise from their graves and aspire
Where my sunflower wishes to go.

The youth and the virgin condemned by the detested One
Law to an existence both spiritually and emotionally barren can
only aspire to the fulfilment of an illusory promise. This poem,
Ah, Sunflower, presents the sole alternative within the world of
Experience to the spiritual devastation expressed in *The Sick
Rose*.

Four poems, *The Little Girl Lost*, *The Little Girl Found*, *The
Voice of the Ancient Bard* and *The Schoolboy*, originally included in
Songs of Innocence, were later transferred to *Songs of Experience* by
Blake. It is easy to see why he made the change.

At first glance *The Little Girl Lost* and *Found* appear to invite
comparison with *Night* in *Songs of Innocence*. But in fact it is the
contrast with that true Song of Innocence that is remarkable.
Indeed *The Little Girl Lost* and *Found* deal in symbolic-narrative
form with more or less the same theme as *Ah, Sunflower*—
chastity and the translation of virtue to a heavenly existence.

In *The Little Girl Lost* the prophetic eye initially looks out
from Experience. It is as if Blake has not yet realised the irremedi-
able tragedy of this organised Experience along the banks of the
Thames, with Urizen himself 'God of all this dreadful ruin', for
he promises 'a garden mild' when earth arises from sleep. The
promise is, of course, realms away from the hills and valleys of
Innocence, which are irrecoverable. It is no more than solace, the
kind of comfort Enitharmon allows.

Chastity and virginity, though both lauded and lost with
repetitive readiness in pastoral verse, are never mentioned in
Songs of Innocence. If we have comprehended Innocence, we

should never expect the words 'maid' or 'maiden' to occur, and they do not. Now, in *The Little Girl Lost*, beneath the moonlit, 'frowning night',

> Sleeping Lyca lay
> While the beasts of prey,
> Come from caverns deep,
> Viewed the maid alseep.
>
> The kingly lion stood
> And the virgin viewed,
> Then he gambolled round
> O'er the hallowed ground.

Instead of reconciliation, the vocabulary establishes a relationship that is personal yet distant; emotion is sublimated into reverence. The triumph of Lyca over the lion is based upon the mythical power of chastity commonplace in literature—'the sage observation that a lion would never hurt a true virgin'. Blake uses this piece of folklore to disquieting effect. There is neither Innocence nor love in *The Little Girl Lost* and *Found*, but only humble devotion and solicitude, and these belong to Experience. Royal solicitude feeds on humble devotion.

The poems seem to be carried along on treacherous undercurrents of meaning, of intangible direction and depth. The allegory will not conform to a neat re-statement. Lyca the child is the lost victim, and also the virgin adored. The devoted attention of the lioness brings to the child a menacing defencelessness and leads to the cavern:

> While the lioness
> Loosed her slender dress,
> And naked they conveyed
> To caves the sleeping maid.

The formality of the poem's address is rare in Blake, and has a venerable odour. The beasts move in a measured ritual through a visionary, stylised landscape. The lion is both kingly and profoundly reverential. In *The Little Girl Found* the 'benevolence'

129

of royal 'protection' is identified in the lion of pride. Moreover, he is given divine authority in parental eyes, becoming 'a spirit armed in gold'. The parents rejoice to find Lyca asleep and join her secluded existence in the 'palace deep' in 'a lonely dell'.

As we read this poem we are aware of the shadows of Urizen moving across the mind. The tenuous implications drift in the subconscious acquisitions of a thousand years of doctrine and myth.

Now *Nurse's Song*, for instance, in *Songs of Experience* is clearly contrary to its counterpart in Innocence:

> When the voices of children are heard on the green
> And whisperings are in the dale,
> The days of my youth rise fresh in my mind,
> My face turns green and pale.
>
> Then come home, my children, the sun is gone down,
> And the dews of night arise;
> Your spring and your day are wasted in play,
> And your winter and night in disguise.

The *Little Girl* poems are no less contrary to Innocence. The difference is only less obvious because we too readily equate the virtue of chastity, having worshipped it so long, with the grace of Innocence that is killed in the worshipping. And the foster-care in the *Little Girl* poems belongs to Experience. The child is at once stripped, protected, revered and withdrawn. The contrast with the nurturing on 'the echoing green' is absolute, and it is a telling comment on the bringing up of children in any age and land.

v

The *Introduction* to *Songs of Experience* and *Earth's Answer* were anticipated briefly in the first two stanzas of *The Little Girl Lost*:

> In futurity
> I prophetic see
> That the earth from sleep
> (Grave the sentence deep)

Shall arise and seek
For her maker meek,
And the desert wild
Become a garden mild.

The earth is *condemned* to sleep, and will arise from the sentence, not to greens and meadows, but to a garden—inevitably separate, walled and 'watered in fears'. This 'sentence' of sleep is akin to the 'slumberous mass' in the *Introduction*:

Hear the voice of the Bard!
Who present, past and future sees;
Whose ears have heard
The Holy Word
That walked among the ancient trees

Calling the lapsed soul,
And weeping in the evening dew;
That might control
The starry pole,
And fallen, fallen light renew!

'O Earth, O Earth, return!
Arise from out the dewy grass;
Night is worn,
And the morn
Rises from the slumberous mass.

'Turn away no more;
Why wilt thou turn away?
The starry floor,
The watery shore,
Is given thee till the break of day.'

The essential key to this poem is that it is not a clarion call to the 'lapsed soul' to return to a state of Innocence. The Bard is perhaps best understood as Blake himself—but the Blake of *Songs of Experience*. With ironic emphasis, we are asked to listen to the prophet who has heeded 'the Holy Word', which dwelt in the 'ancient trees' (the forests of affliction, of superstition and darkness), which weeps hypocritical tears 'in the evening dew', which calls the earth to awake to the dawn of an allegorical after-life, and which offers sensual consolation under the repressive edicts of this life.

It is essential to recognise the irony in the *Introduction* to make *Earth's Answer* comprehensible. In *Earth's Answer*, written before the *Introduction*, Blake looks from a different angle at the starry night of 'woman's secrecy' and 'soft delusion', and its relation to the Holy Word among the forests that overwhelm Innocence. It is simply the victim's way of looking at the holy conspiracy between Urizen's 'starry jealousy' and the 'woman's secrecy' taught by Enitharmon. It is the conspiracy that leads the soul into caverns, no matter if they seem indulgent palaces. The Earth recognises Urizen's voice in the Holy Word, and asks the question that Oothoon puts, and Theotormon dare not face, in *Visions of the Daughters of Albion*:

> Selfish Father of men!
> Cruel, jealous, selfish fear!
> Can delight,
> Chained in night,
> The virgins of youth and morning bear?

Like Oothoon, the Earth demands release from 'the heavy chain' 'that free Love with bondage bound'. Once again, we must read the phrase 'free Love' in a spiritual, intellectual and physical sense; it is love intuitive, selfless and creative, uncompelled by a social code. It is not promiscuity, and it is not exclusively sexual. And to avoid the old error of making Blake the advocate of universal licence, it is worth recollecting that he called each act of adultery and fornication 'some stinking weed'.

The Earth 'chained in night' is held in bondage at the most intimate level, in the reactions of the curtained soul; but these reactions emanate to manifest themselves in human relationships and to shape society. The child in *Infant Sorrow* tells how his parents, governed by Urizen, induce his sullen hatred:

> Struggling in my father's hands,
> Striving against my swaddling-bands,
> Bound and weary I thought best
> To sulk upon my mother's breast.

Society, fashioning Christianity to its own purposes, had bound the infant Christ in just such swaddling-bands; Blake recollects the familiar account of the Nativity.

In *A Poison Tree*, it is anger which is nursed in the garden of Experience, and which is subtly transformed into temptation, and then to death:

> In the morning glad I see
> My foe outstretched beneath the tree.

In *The Human Abstract* Blake traces the sequence back from the social condition, where the existence of poverty and misery are justified with a welcome casuistry—

> Pity would be no more
> If we did not make somebody poor;
> And mercy no more would be
> If all were as happy as we.

—derived from the 'tree of mystery' that grows 'in the human brain'. The power that holds the inhabitants of London's 'chartered streets' in the 'petrific abominable chaos' alongside 'the chartered Thames' is the more potent for being invisible and intangible, and forged in the intellect:

> In every cry of every man,
> In every infant's cry of fear,
> In every voice, in every ban,
> The mind-forged manacles I hear.

Even in *London*, the most direct condemnation Blake wrote of 'the terrible desert' in which he lived, he still identifies the roots of misery and evil in a way of thought to some extent self-inflicted, certainly acquired, as it were, with the air an infant breathed. And so complete is the way of thought that it has become 'a divine image', hardened in the human form as if in a furnace.

The furious revolt against all this is given shape in *The Tiger*. It is a measure of the stature of this poem that it has been recognised as incomparable, even when it has been misunderstood and under-rated. Incredibly, *The Tiger* was seen by James Thomson in 1884 as 'a magnificent expression of boyish wonder and admiring terror', and by Alice Meynell, as late as 1927, as 'a Sunday-school poem for children':

> Tiger! Tiger! burning bright
> In the forests of the night,
> What immortal hand or eye
> Could frame thy fearful symmetry?
>
> In what distant deeps or skies
> Burnt the fire of thine eyes?
> On what wings dare he aspire?
> What the hand dare seize the fire?
>
> And what shoulder, and what art,
> Could twist the sinews of thy heart?
> And when thy heart began to beat,
> What dread hand? and what dread feet?
>
> What the hammer? what the chain?
> In what furnace was thy brain?
> What the anvil? what dread grasp
> Dare its deadly terrors clasp?
>
> When the stars threw down their spears,
> And watered heaven with their tears,
> Did he smile his work to see?
> Did he who made the Lamb make thee?
>
> Tiger! Tiger! burning bright
> In the forests of the night,
> What immortal hand or eye
> Dare frame thy fearful symmetry?

The Tiger is a symbol of spiritual revolt backed by uninhibited natural energy. It is unique in Blake's poetry, as the only example of a symbol created within the scope of a single brief poem; and it gathers into its meaning much of the force of what Blake has said in the Lambeth Books. Part of the poem's meaning lies in its incessant, intense sinewy beat—a firmness that contrasts absolutely with the spacious movement in *Night*, with its symbol of the lion of royal pride.

134

The poem extends into realm beyond realm of meaning. 'The forests of the night' are the 'vast forests' of Urizen, 'shut in the deep' (*Urizen* I, 5). To be sure, the word 'deeps' was a commonplace metaphor for time and space in the 18th century; but when Blake adopts it he transforms it by putting it alongside 'skies'. These are the overwhelming, obliterating seas, which Urizen, this 'cloudy god, seated on waters', calls 'my deep, my night'. Here the Tiger is created (as was that other revolutionary figure, Orc), and these are the obscure spaces he illuminates.

Against the vast depth and distance we have a concentration upon the particular part of the creator (eye, hand, shoulder, for instance) relevant to the creation. The control is exact, and the 'symmetry' of the Tiger is not only named, but is realised in this control.

Blake gives the word 'art' the maximum weight. He often associated the word with prolonged labour, and the production of some challenging artifact. In *Jerusalem* I, 11, we learn how Los 'compelled the invisible spectre'

> To labours mighty with vast strength, with his mighty chains,
> In pulsations of time, and extensions of space . . .
> With great labour upon his anvils, and in his ladles the ore
> He lifted, pouring it into the clay ground prepared with art.

As our imagination concentrates on the limbs, actions and implements of the immortal blacksmith, the intensity of the physical action deepens, and the Tiger is no longer a fire in the forests of eternity, but meets mankind. The sinews of revolt are knotted into existence.

Without the fifth stanza, *The Tiger* would have had a more obvious unity. The imagination had travelled from the forests of night into the glowing forge of creation, making a compact poem rounded off by a repetition of the initial stanza. But the stanza of the Lamb extends the vision once more to the infinity of night, and adds a dimension to the poem. And after this the concluding stanza is no mere repetition. It derives new meaning from its context.

By now we recognise the stars as symbolic of the malignant forces of oppression, of the spreading of pestilence, and of overweening pride. They are 'the starry hosts' led by Urizen, and here the spears of strife are thrown aside and pity is assumed. And the Creator, no longer Los or Urizen but the God of Innocence, smiles upon the triumph of the Lamb.

The symbol of the stars throwing aside the spears expresses the triumph of Inspiration and Innocence over Experience, and the magination moves here, as it has done already in earlier stanzas, from the spatial theme to the deed of creation—the handiwork:

Did he smile his work to see?
Did he who made the Lamb make thee?

Inspiration and Innocence are like waters from one fountain. It is something Blake has been trying to get across so often.

8

Towards Jerusalem

In 1794, by the time Blake was thirty-seven, almost all his poetry of undisputed greatness had been written. In the Lambeth Books themselves there is already evidence of an increasing preoccupation with an esoteric mythology that is puzzling rather than challenging. In 1797 he began *Vala, or The Four Zoas*. Blake once more writes against war and in condemnation of the dominant spiritual evil in which wars are generated. He prefaced the poem with a quotation from *Ephesians*: 'For our contention is not with the blood and the flesh, but with dominion, with authority, with the blind world-rulers of this life, with the spirit of evil in things heavenly.' *The Four Zoas* is formidably difficult, and can only be followed from a detailed knowledge of contemporary events, to which Blake adapted his attitude as he wrote. Even the scheme of Nine Nights into which he sets the tenuous theme is no guide. The poem was abandoned in manuscript. One can only suggest that the reader will find in it passages of great poetry interspersed with baffling exegesis.

In 1797 also, Blake's illustrations of Young's *Night Thoughts* (where he found the framework for *The Four Zoas*) proved a commercial failure and work was not easy for him to find after this.

By July 2, 1800, he was writing to George Cumberland: 'I begin to emerge from a deep pit of melancholy, melancholy without any real reason for it, a disease which God keep you from, and all good men . . . I have been too little among friends . . .'

About the same time he wrote the poem *To Tirzah* which was put with later copies of *Songs of Experience*:

What e'er is born of mortal birth
Must be consumed with the earth
To rise from generation free:
Then what have I to do with thee?

The sexes sprung from shame and pride,
Blowed in the morn, in evening died;
But Mercy changed death into sleep,
The sexes rose to work and weep.

Thou, mother of my mortal part,
With cruelty didst mould my heart,
And with false self-deceiving tears
Didst bind my nostrils, eyes and ears,

Didst close my tongue in senseless clay,
And me to mortal life betray.
The death of Jesus set me free:
Then what have I to do with thee?

The change in style and theme and the unprecedented Christian emphasis are at once apparent. The biblical Tirzah was a city in Canaan, and Blake uses it often in his final books, together with Rahab, as the antithesis to Jerusalem. It represented the spirit of moral repression that governed the Asylum for Female Orphans in what should have been

> Jerusalem's Inner Court, Lambeth, ruined and given
> To the detestable Gods of Priam, to Apollo, and at the Asylum
> Given to Hercules, who labour in Tirzah's Looms for bread.
>
> MILTON, 27

In September 1800 Blake took the opportunity offered by an invitation from William Hayley, the poet and landed gentleman, to move from the spiritual ruins of Lambeth to Felpham in Sussex. He was to be employed illustrating Hayley's work, and arrived at the cottage overlooking the sea, 'a perfect model for cottages', with high hopes, finding that 'Felpham is a sweet place for study, because it is more spiritual than London. Heaven opens here on all sides her golden gates. Her windows are not obstructed by vapours'. In May 1801 he was inviting Thomas Butts and Mrs. Butts to Felpham, 'the sweetest spot on earth'. But it did not last. By January of 1802 he was writing to Butts that he was ill and that 'the ague and rheumatism' had been Catherine's 'constant enemies . . . ever since we have been here'. Soon he had determined 'to leave Felpham entirely', and by July 1803 he was finding Hayley 'much averse' to his poetry, and was 'determined to be no longer pestered with his genteel ignorance and polite disapprobation'.

Besides the other annoyances at Felpham, Blake found himself faced with a charge of sedition when a soldier, John Schofield, whom he had turned out of his garden, 'swore that he heard me D—n the K—g'.

It was an obscure affair, and though Blake protested his innocence, Schofield put words into his mouth that voiced opinions he certainly held in secret.

Blake was charged with 'wickedly and seditiously intending to bring our said Lord, the King, into great hatred, contempt and scandal . . . and intending to withdraw the fidelity and allegiance of his said Majesty's subjects . . .' Blake was acquitted by the jury, despite a hostile summary from the judge, the Duke of Richmond, at the assizes at Chichester in January 1804. The public in the court cheered the verdict.

By this time Blake had been back in London for four months living at 17 South Molton Street, half a mile west of Broad Street. He had achieved the move, he was happy to say, with Hayley's approbation. Indeed soon after arriving in town Blake wrote to thank Hayley for his 'generous and tender solicitude', and went on to complain:

How is it possible that a man almost 50 years of age, who has not lost any of his life since he was five years old without incessant labour and study, how is it possible that such a one with ordinary common sense can be inferior to a boy of twenty, who scarcely has taken or deigns to take pencil in hand, but who rides about the Parks or saunters about the Playhouses, who eats and drinks for business not for need—how is it possible that such a fop can be superior to the studious lover of Art can scarcely be imagined. Yet such is somewhat like my fate and such it is likely to remain. Yet I laugh and sing, for if on earth neglected, I am in heaven a Prince among Princes, and even on earth beloved of the good as a good man . . . O that I could live as others do in a regular succession of employment, this wish I fear is not to be accomplished to me—forgive this dirge-like lamentation over a dead horse. And now I have lamented over the dead horse let me laugh and be merry with my friends till Christmas, for as man liveth not by bread alone, I shall live although I should want bread.

There is much in that letter of both Blake's character and predicament. During the next two decades he was increasingly dependent on his friends for the means of livelihood. Any material prosperity he had enjoyed was now past, though his needs were seemingly slight.

During these years war seemed the sole prospect for Englishmen caught 'in laws and deceitful religions' that committed the country to famine and the manufacture of armaments. 'Urizen, in self-deceit, his warlike preparations fabricated.'

Horrible hooks and nets he formed, twisting the cords of iron
And brass, and molten metals cast in hollow globes and bored
Tubes in petrific steel and rammed combustibles and wheels
And chains and pulleys fabricated.

'In the work of death,' he brought out

all his engines of deceit, that linked chains might run
Through ranks of war spontaneous, and that locks and boring screws

might be ready 'to grate the soul with destruction.' (*The Four Zoas* VIII)

Mainly in the four years after his return to London, Blake wrote *Milton*. His experience at Chichester Assizes had strengthened his caution, and the mythological maze around his

140

dangerous recommendations becomes if anything more deeply impenetrable. It faces the reader with such an effort of detection that he reaches the poetry exhausted. And yet paradoxically the opening verses, beginning 'And did those feet in ancient time', are so universally known that they need not be quoted. 'The sick father and his starving family' and 'the prisoner in the stone dungeon and the slave at the mill' during these years of 'sighs and heart broken lamentations' hardly knew England as a 'green and pleasant land'. The 'dark satanic mills' dominated London both spiritually and materially, and the intellectual revolt symbolised in the 'bow of burning gold' and the 'arrows of desire' would have to be fierce indeed to build Jerusalem among these ruins.

When Blake wrote *Jerusalem* itself, his final long poem, in some respects a revision of *The Four Zoas*, he was still engaged fundamentally in recalling Albion from war and 'the shades of death'. But by now, for all the continuing and self-evident misery, Blake's neighbourhood in North London was the scene of much rebuilding. As he said in *Jerusalem* 38:

> I write in South Moulton Street what I both see and hear
> In regions of humanity, in London's opening streets.

When Blake was writing *Jerusalem* in the years approaching 1820, John Nash was opening the way between Westminster and his mansions in Regent's Park by building Regent Street along the mean line of ancient Swallow Street. Before the new street was laid, a coach could take almost an hour to reach the House of Commons from Portland Place. John Nash's vast undertaking in dusty demolition and construction went on a few yards east of Blake's home. By the summer of 1819 the new street was opened as far as Piccadilly.

Once more, while Blake writes of Jerusalem being built, it would seem to be happening around him. And one point must be made in this respect, as it is relevant indirectly to *Songs of Innocence*.

141

There is a passage in the first interchapter of *Jerusalem* that is often quoted:

> The fields from Islington to Marylebone,
> To Primrose Hill and St. John's Wood,
>   Were builded over with pillars of gold,
> And there Jerusalem's pillars stood.
>
> Her little ones ran on the fields,
> The Lamb of God among them seen,
>   And fair Jerusalem, his Bride,
> Among the little meadows green.
>
> Pancras and Kentish Town repose
> Among her gold pillars high,
>   Among her golden arches which
> Shine upon the starry sky.
>
> The Jew's Harp House and the Green Man,
> The ponds where boys to bathe delight,
>   The fields of cows by Willan's Farm,
> Shine in Jerusalem's pleasant sight.
>
> What are those golden builders doing
> Near mournful, ever-weeping Paddington,
>   Standing above that mighty ruin
> Where Satan the first victory won,
>
> Where Albion slept beneath the Fatal Tree,
> And the Druid's golden knife
>   Rioted in human gore,
> In offerings of human life?
>
> They groaned aloud on London Stone,
> They groaned aloud on Tyburn's Brook,
>   Albion gave his deadly groan,
> And all the Atlantic mountains shook.

In the fifth stanza Blake is approving the buildings going up on the 'extensive waste' that was Paddington, 'occupied with the most wretched huts'. Here the Grand Junction Canal ended in Paddington Basin, where crowds of casual labourers found work, and John Nash was busy extending the canal through Marylebone, and round his Park. The Regent's Canal was finished in 1820. To the west, Nash's 'golden builders' were working over the 'mighty ruin' of Tyburn, and 'London Stone' was the stone at Tyburn marked on John Rocque's map in 1745 as 'the Stone where soldiers are shot'. Blake had met the Ancient Order of Druids long ago; indeed its revival took place in 1781 in the old King's Arms in Poland Street. Now he associated Druidism with false religion and the loss of Jerusalem; its sacrificial altar was the Stone at Tyburn. So at last here is Jerusalem being built where the ancient gallows stood.

Critics invariably read into the first four verses an idyllic recollection of Blake's boyhood. They would have the meadows to the north of Tyburn Road (Oxford Street) a heaven for any boy, and the young Blake is seen wandering to Pancras past Paradise Row and 'through the pastures called Lamb's Conduit Fields, east of the Green Man'. The difficulty is that in Lamb's Conduit Fields at the back of the Foundling Hospital were buried many of the soldiers who 'were shot'. And to get through these 'pastures' a boy had to walk either through this burial ground, across Gravel Pit Field, or through 'Mr. Mullet's Bowling Green'. Any way, he came to paddocks, brickfields, cow-lays, ponds and inevitably the mountainous dust heap (they drove carts up it and round its base) at Battle Bridge, Pancras; yet,

Pancras and Kentish Town repose
Among her golden pillars high.

Clearly something is wrong with the notion that these are evocative recollections of the poet's youth. Moreover, Blake himself wrote to John Linnell in 1826 that when he was young 'all the places north of London' always laid him up with a 'torment of the stomach', 'lasting sometimes two or three days'.

Blake never equates his childhood with either Innocence or Jerusalem. Quite apart from the fact that this reading of the

143

verses is historically indefensible (the landscape I have indicated can be extended), we should not misinterpret his meaning so completely. Here again, Blake is looking at London around him, and again his vision is synoptic.

Blake never sought natural solitude as the idyllic life. For him indeed, 'where man is not, nature is barren'. In writing of Jerusalem, he demands a rebuilding of the city. It is not Innocence, and certainly not his boyhood. When he writes of the 'pillars of gold' and 'the golden builders' he is looking at the whole development that seemed to be transforming suburban villages, royal domains and waste lands into a Jerusalem, while *Jerusalem* was being written. The farms (Willan's and two others) stood in the Crown Estate of Marylebone (now Regent's) Park, the boys bathed in the ponds, while all around Nash's building went on. The project of building magnificently in the royal park had been cherished and talked of since 1793. For twenty years Blake must have known of it, before Nash put up his plan. By 1816 the roads and ornamental basin were laid. During the next three years, as Blake was writing *Jerusalem*, villas went up in the fields, Park Crescent was being built and Macclesfield Bridge carried the road across the water on Doric columns. The first of Nash's great terraces was not occupied till 1827, but before 1820, to the east, he had built Albany Street and Cumberland Market. And other builders were at work, notably in Lamb's Conduit Fields—the area round present-day Cromer Street. Cottages, houses and mansions were going up all round, in the brickfields and on the royal estate, while in the park the ponds and farms survived. So Blake's imagination takes in an ancient Jerusalem, relates it to the immediate moment, and projects it into the future, with a treatment of time typical of him. As always in Blake the stimulus is an immediate circumstance from which the vision radiates. His mind's eye sees the future and the ancient past *through* the present. He said himself that 'imagination has nothing to do with memory'. Least of all in his poetry has it anything to do with nostalgia. And yet, because it makes what he says more easy to take, we persist in reading a personal recollection into a poem where it is not even implied. If we do not see now that we are sharing a vision not a solace, we shall never understand Blake.

But the community of spirit Blake longed to proclaim was as insubstantial as ever. According to Nash, Regent Street was to form 'a boundary and complete separation between the streets and squares occupied by the nobility and gentry, and the narrow streets and meaner houses occupied by mechanics and the trading part of the community'. John Nash was reflecting his age, not building Blake's Jerusalem in London. And Nash's Regent Street still stands, in our minds at least.

In 1821 Blake had to sell his print collection, and moved east into meaner London. From now on he lived in lodgings in Fountain Court, off the Strand, where the friendship of John Linnell went far to keep him alive. During his last years he enjoyed the unexpected adulation of a group of young artists. They seemed to carry Blake into the future.

He never lost either his wit or his rebellious insistence upon the life of the spirit. Having lost weight in his long illness he told Linnell that he could not 'start for Hampstead like a young lark without feathers', and in August 1826 he was 'still incapable of riding in a Stage and shall be, I fear, for some time being only bones and sinews, all strings and bobbins like a weaver's loom'. By April 12, 1827, he had been 'very near the gates of death', and had returned 'very weak and an old man, feeble and tottering, but not in spirit and life, not in the real man, the imagination, which liveth for ever'. Four months to the day from his death he was still rebellious: 'Since the French Revolution Englishmen are all intermeasurable by one another. Certainly a happy state of agreement, in which I for one do not agree.'

And in this same letter to George Cumberland he recalls, now in a quiet way, the long years of furious protest against the laws of oppression:

Flaxman is gone, and we must all soon follow, every one to his own Eternal House, leaving the delusive Goddess Nature and her laws, to get to the freedom from all law of the Members, into the Mind, in which everyone is King and Priest in his own house. God send it so on earth, as it is in heaven.

Blake died on August 12, 1827, singing at the top of his voice. Catherine lived another four years. One who knew her said that she returned a gift of £100 sent her by Princess Sophia, because others were in greater need. True or not, it is the right finish.

A typical page from Blake's *Notebook* (B.M. Additional 49460)

9

Blake's Earlier Critics

i

The first commentary on Blake's poetry was to call it insane. The verdict had been reached in the columns of Leigh Hunt's *Examiner* for August 7, 1808, and September 17, 1809, and it was about this time that Blake, 'this insane and erratic genius', 'showed Southey a perfectly mad poem called *Jerusalem*' (H. Crabb Robinson, *Diary, Reminiscences and Correspondence*, ed. T. Sadler, 1869, I, 338). In 1833 Edward FitzGerald, who had got hold of a copy of *Songs of Innocence*, was interesting himself in the poet 'from the strangeness of the constitution of his mind'— a 'genius with a screw loose' (Edward FitzGerald, *Letters*, 1894, I, 25–6).

However, it was usual to except *Songs of Innocence* from the charge of madness. The *Songs* were Blake's saving grace for most people, among them J. G. Wilkinson, Blake's first editor. When Wilkinson brought out his edition of *Songs of Innocence and of Experience* in 1839, a volume, he said, 'which contains nearly all that is excellent in Blake's poetry' (xx), he wrote guardedly about the 'darker themes' in *Songs of Experience*, and complained of the 'wildness and fierce vagary', the 'madness', in most of Blake's work, adding that 'no madness can long be considered either really Poetic or Artistical' (xvii–xviii).

The first biography was Alexander Gilchrist's *Life of William Blake*. D. G. Rossetti had taken over the unpublished papers on Gilchrist's death in 1861, and the biography came out two years later. The achievement of Gilchrist and Rossetti (quite apart from

Rossetti's preservation of the famous *Notebook*) was considerable. The magazines began to notice Blake and his writings. Following the lead given by Gilchrist, Swinburne was forthright about Blake's 'madness' in his *Critical Essay* (1868): 'Let all readers and all critics get rid of that notion for good . . . in these strangest of all written books there is purpose as well as power, meaning as well as mystery' (185–6).

Six years later Swinburne was for W. M. Rossetti (*The Poetical Works of William Blake*, cxix, cxxi) 'the only one who has ever conned these works without being bewildered and stunned, and hounded into desperation'. Rossetti 'confessed his own opinion' that the Prophetic Books 'are, taken as a whole, neither readable nor wholly sane performances'.

It was in 1921 that Geoffrey Keynes made the telling point at last about Blake's letters: 'If read consecutively they will be found to bring out clearly his peculiar and unstable mentality; but at the same time it is clear that anyone who could deal so normally with the ordinary affairs of life as the writer of these letters cannot be regarded as a madman in the usual sense of the word' (*A Bibliography of William Blake*, New York, 1921, 6–7).

The question seemed to fascinate critics, leading their pens into contradictory nonsense. In 1911 Alice Meynell wrote, 'Today a man of letters who should roundly call Blake a madman would be thought to have cast away his literary reputation', adding within a few lines the qualification that at the same time 'Blake's intellect did, terribly and portentously, overpass the limits of normal sanity', and even going on to use the 'insanity' she had denied as 'proof' of the poet's genius: 'Blake's genius is, in fact, entangled with his insanity. A sign and proof of the purity and singleness of that genius is precisely that it is entangled with his high insanity, and with nothing else' (*Poems by William Blake*, iii–iv).

This twofold story of 'another fine mind dethroned', yet of a man 'really great when he is content with imaginative images and can haunt our imaginations' (Osbert Burdett, *William Blake*, 1926, 65, 48)—this naïve approach was the easy path which led to the paradoxical logic of A. E. Housman's Leslie Stephen Lecture (1933). According to Housman, the only true poets of the 18th century were Collins, Christopher Smart, Cowper and Blake. 'And what other characteristic had these four in common? They were mad.' To Housman it was Blake's greatest poetic asset. It made him 'the most poetical of all poets', because it guaranteed that what he wrote was meaningless, 'so that we can listen with all our hearing to his celestial tune' (*The Name and Nature of Poetry*, 38–40).

Blake's 'madness' led to this critical dead-end. It is strange how unintelligently, persistently and recently the track was followed. The real criticism of Blake is a different story.

ii

When in 1818 Coleridge listed some of Blake's poems in order of merit, he apparently preferred those that expressed a moral orthodoxy, and if he discussed a poem he did so from the doctrinal point of view ('Coleridge on Blake's Songs', by B. R. McElderry Jnr. in *Modern Language Quarterly*, vol. 9, no. 3, 298–302). Moral tone was important. More sympathetic to Blake's meaning, if too hopeful of dawning optimism, J. G. Wilkinson was soon conscious of defending Blake against Allan Cunningham and his 'Mercantile Ethics', saying (op. cit. xii, xxi), 'We have been sedulous to exclude from our pages, his tone of feeling, and style of thought, in speaking of Blake; for we have found him incapable, by Nature or by Will, of dealing with the Spiritual phenomena, of which that extraordinary person was the subject and exhibiter'. Wilkinson was content if his edition gave 'one impulse to the New Spiritualism which is now dawning on the world'.

In his edition of *Songs of Innocence and Experience with other Poems* (1866) R. H. Shepherd, following Gilchrist closely, made an early attempt to relate Blake to other poets. He saw the lyrics as important in the 'history' of English Literature, Blake being 'the first to inaugurate the return to simplicity and nature in his poetry', and pointed to 'the remarkable resemblance in tone and style, the similarities of subject and metre, between these poems and the earlier poems of Wordsworth . . . There is precisely the same exquisite tenderness and noble simplicity in Blake' (ix–x). Shepherd found Blake's 'perfection of lyrical expression' 'unequalled except in Shakespeare and Tennyson', and although it means so little, it is refreshing to find Blake treated as another poet rather than as an oddity, refreshing to hear the comfortable terms applied to his faults—his imperfect number of feet, uncertain ear, failing in rhyme and want of 'additional polish'. The method had already descended to the periodicals where, among the commonplace stories, invented and true, of Blake's affairs, we find his poetry compared with Coleridge's, Cowper's, Wordsworth's, Burns's, Shelley's and Tennyson's.

iii

With Swinburne's *William Blake, A Critical Essay* (1868) we have the first major shift in evaluation, and *Songs of Experience* are preferred: 'In the *Songs of Innocence* there is no such glory of metre or sonorous beauty of lyrical work as here' (119). Swinburne first saw the value of correlating Blake's books, and even touched upon the link between *Songs of Experience* and the Prophetic Books. But this, perhaps the most valuable of all critical hints, was never followed up by Swinburne or taken up by anyone else until my own *Infinity on the Anvil* (1954). Moreover, Swinburne walked the edge of the symbolic country explored in that book almost a century later. He saw Urizen as 'God of cloud and star . . . the types of mystery and distance, of cold alienation and heavenly jealousy . . . even as the spirit of revolt is made manifest in fiery incarnation—pure prolific fire' (192–3). Despite this awareness, *Europe* and *America* were 'divine babble' amid 'chaotic and Titanic scenery' (196), and *Urizen* 'perhaps more chaotic at a first glimpse than any other of these prose poems' (246). At least the longer poems were discussed. And Swinburne thought *The Marriage of Heaven and Hell* the greatest of all Blake's books, 'a work indeed which we rank as about the greatest produced by the 18th century in the line of high poetry and spiritual speculation' (204). We might not go as far as that now; but *The Marriage* has been put high among Blake's writings ever since.

We suspect Swinburne's eye when he writes of *Songs of Innocence*: 'Such a fiery outbreak of spring, such an insurrection of fierce floral life and radiant riot of childish power and pleasure, no poet or painter ever gave before.' By contrast, W. M. Rossetti in his edition of *The Poetical Works* (1874) puts it differently: 'Some of the little poems included in this series are the most perfect expression ever given . . . to babe-life—to what a man can remember of himself as an infant, or can enter into as existing in other infants, or can love as of the essence of infancy' (cxvi).

'The divine voice of childhood' lulled readers for years. For James Thomson *The Tiger* was 'a magnificent expression of boyish wonder and terror' (*Essay on . . . Blake*, 1884, 115), which may or may not be the same as saying that 'none so early as 1794 came so near to the heart of Romanticism as Blake in poems like *The Tiger*' (*The Prophetic Writings*, ed. Sloss and Wallis, 1926, II, 103), or that the poem is 'a Sunday-school poem for children, and it is in the crown of English Literature' (*Poems*, ed. Alice Meynell, 1927, viii). This over-simplification of *Experience* led inevitably to the acceptance of the poems as 'magic', and to critical despair that persisted well into the present century.

However, not all commentators read Blake's poetry so unthinkingly. After Gilchrist and Swinburne, who first hinted at symbolism, the next great influence in Blake studies was *The Works of William Blake, Poetic, Symbolic and Critical*, edited by E. J. Ellis and W. B. Yeats in 1893. This was elaborate and massive, an impressive failure. From 1893, however, Blake studies went two ways. Commentators either trailed after the mythology in the longer books, or they hedged themselves within the 'simple' plots of the 'lyrics'. It was 1954 before the two tracks met again.

It is revealing that even in their title Ellis and Yeats separated the 'works symbolic' from the 'poetic'. (This predicted the future of Blake studies.) They went to great lengths to elucidate the mythology; and the fog of analogy, philosophy and sources thickens along the way. Urizen, 'Blake's greatest dramatisation', is 'god both of intellectual and material light. The separation of the cold light beam from the warm flame is a symbol of his descent into matter, a symbolism found also in Swedenborg' (I, 252–3).

The discussion of the mythology led away from the poetry, mainly towards the sources, most persistent of which was (wrongly) seen as Swedenborg. (In effect, his influence on Blake was transient.) And Ellis and Yeats explained the poetic symbolism, when they touched upon it, by over-simplifying it, or relying upon generalisations that were unjustifiable: 'the sun . . . is especially . . . the symbol of Los and Urizen' (I, 269). And the symbols are discussed outside their contexts.

When Yeats alone brought out an edition of Blake's poems in 1893 he first suggested the continuity from *Poetical Sketches* to the later poetry, and saw the *Sketches* as more than simply imitations of 18th-century verse. Yet Yeats still advises that 'the essentials of the teaching of the Prophetic Books can be best explained by extracts mainly from the prose writings, for the language of the books themselves is exceedingly technical' (xxxv–vi).

Yeats made hardly any critical assessment and this tendency to seek the meaning of the poems in other writings gained momentum steadily after the '90s and more than anything except the mythology led critics to attempt to solve the poems as riddles. It was this desire for a key to Blake, together with a chronic lack of confidence in the poetic symbolism, that put *The Marriage of Heaven and Hell* in such high esteem. So the 'study of Blake's teaching' (still his *teaching* not his poetry) 'begins with *The Marriage of Heaven and Hell*', wrote Sloss and Wallis, adding the illuminating reason that 'the work is almost free from symbolism' (op. cit., ii, 5). By 'symbolism' they understood 'mythology', which they recognised as 'a deliberately cryptic jargon' (ii, iii). But the commentators failed to resist the hypnosis they recognised even after T. S. Eliot made his remark of Blake's 'supernatural territories' in *The Sacred Wood* (1920) that 'they are not essential to Blake's inspiration'—and went on in this brilliant essay to ignore them.

By 1927, two years after Geoffrey Keynes edited *The Writings*, it could be said that 'at the present moment Blake and his mysticism are very live issues' (Helen C. White, *The Mysticism of William Blake*, 21) and it was in this decade that notes on Blake began to proliferate through the learned journals. The academic industry had begun.

In 1924 S. Foster Damon's *William Blake, his Philosophy and Symbols* was published. It was by far the most important book on Blake yet produced. Starting from the view that the 'great part' of Blake criticism was 'worthless' he 'fell back on tracing Blake's very definite system of symbols and on uncovering his literary sources' (vii). Damon anticipated the critics who have since related Blake to his own 'queer and fascinating' century (13). At times he identified the mythology from the symbolism, and indicated at last what he meant by a symbol: 'In the first case [simile] Love would be likened to a rose; in the second case [metaphor] Love would be called a rose; in the third [symbol] the Rose would appear unexplained' (65). Damon pointed to the general significance of the major symbols, and saw that 'Blake had a horror of fixed symbols', adding that 'clouds may be focuses of power or obscurers of truth' (68). Perhaps strangely, however, he did not pursue the importance of the context, and of qualifications offered by Blake. And Damon's technique of isolating a symbol, besides not leading to a critical conclusion, often restricted Blake's meaning.

In 1932 a facsimile of *Visions of the Daughters of Albion* was published in New York, with a note by J. Middleton Murry—a note in the tradition of philosophic interpretation. Murry was no longer concerned, as Ellis and Yeats had been, at the surface of the poems 'perpetually, as it were, giving way before one' (op. cit., I, 287), and he no longer sought a mythological system. He accepted the poetic nature of the writing—'the nature of things requires this passing and repassing into clarity. Therefore,

I think, we need to be on our guard against those learned and well-meaning persons who would systematise Blake's symbols' (14). The warning was timely. Then in 1933 Murry published his *William Blake*, written solely to expound 'the *doctrine* of William Blake'. The preoccupation with doctrine continued throughout the years between the wars. It was an interest that neglected the shorter poems. Book followed book from the philosophical critics in their quest along the higher reaches of speculation, and if they descended to *Songs of Innocence and of Experience* at all, it was for no more than a moment.

In 1947 Northrop Frye's *Fearful Symmetry*, written on the assumption that we must perceive, not deduce, Blake's meaning, marked the beginning of the post-war phase of criticism which has brought us much closer to understanding Blake, because it has concentrated on the poetry, as poetry.

iv

During this century the high quality of Blake's long prophecies (*The Four Zoas, Milton* and *Jerusalem*) has been more or less tacitly assumed by the 'serious' critics. Despite this, no one has yet produced a justification of these daunting books, while other editors were presenting the shorter poems to readers of less stamina. Even here, however, we find an increasing awareness that Blake's poetry is more than simply lyrical. As early as 1905, when Sir Walter Raleigh wrote the introduction to *The Lyrical Poems* edited by John Sampson, the Prophetic Books were no longer condemned as chaotic outright, and their chaos contrasted with the lyrics. The remarks of the commentator were much more temperate and convincing, arising from an attitude that was sympathetic. There was a real change in attitude. The Prophetic Books were no longer insane; but they were still not judged as poetry. Following Ellis and Yeats, Raleigh saw them as 'an elaborate cipher' (xv). He doubted whether Blake's 'whole scheme will ever be fully expounded', yet saw its unity, adding that no interpreter who regards it as a series of whimsical, unrelated and fitful utterances dare hope for success' (xiv). Moreover, he was aware of some of Blake's symbolism: 'This dark Satanic mill . . . which overshadows humanity, has woven, for a garment of oppression, the woof and warp of Good and Evil' (xxix).

Basil de Selincourt contradicted Raleigh in his edition of *Selected Poems* (1927): 'Raleigh himself . . . calls Blake's consistency a merit in his thinking though it might better be called its chief defect.' In *Thel* he found 'the mesmeric meanderings . . . of weakness indulged'. There is little to help the reader here. And de Selincourt meets Blake's challenge with easy misapprehension that became a commonplace reaction: 'His wrathful advocacy of free love misleads nobody today.' In Blake's Prophetic Books, de Selincourt saw 'the measure of his weakest faculty, the intellectual' (viii–x).

If we set these pronouncements against a line or two from a later editor, we see how a reader's attitude may change a poet's meaning into a congenial message. It is a salutary warning. What for de Selincourt was a no longer misleading 'wrathful advocacy of free love', was for Lawrence Binyon a hymning of 'the honest pleasures of natural instinct'. Whereas for de Selincourt Blake's weakest faculty was 'the intellectual', Binyon writes that 'Blake's reaction was intellectual rather than moral' (*Poems of Blake*, 1931, xviii, xvi). The danger lies in the attempt to state Blake's philosophy, which sounded so many realms, on a single facile plane. It has taken us a long time to *realise* what Blake is saying.

In biographical writing on Blake, again there has been a tendency to confuse surmise with fact. So writing of *My Pretty Rose-tree* in his *William Blake* (1951) H. M. Margoliouth repeats an assumption that had been made long before. The poem, he said, 'was occasioned by, and records, a marital misunderstanding. A very attractive woman had made advances to Blake, which, as a happily married man, he had rejected. Coming home, very pleased with himself, he told his wife. Instead of praising him for his fidelity, she was angry and jealous . . . The tension lasted some time' (57). And this 'continuous excitement' probably produced *Songs of Experience*.

This sounds well enough, but the only evidence lies in the short poem *My Pretty Rose-tree* itself. The rest is surmise. And the biographies are not unanimous on the happiness of Blake's marriage. S. F. Damon relates that Blake 'was ideally married' (op. cit., 99). Kathleen Raine (*William Blake*, 1951) says that Catherine Blake, 'the illiterate daughter of a market gardener', was 'one of the exemplary wives of literary history'. However, Bernard Blackstone observes that 'probably no man has regretted his marriage more, though his biographers tend to gloss this over, and make out that the match was little short of idyllic' (*English Blake*, 1949, 7).

The standard *Life* of Blake was written by Mona Wilson, and appeared in 1932. It remains a valuable commentary, though it has now been superseded in many respects by D. V. Erdman's book of immense scholarship, *Blake: Prophet against Empire* (1954), in which Blake's poetry, often line by line, is related to contemporary events. This historical approach has gone far to 'approximate Blake's own perspective'. He no longer stands as an isolated crank. We are shown the reason behind Blake's complex allegory. Yet the approach, as it were, catches everything up in its own momentum. The historical analysis often leads us astray in its assumptions. And we are sometimes guided away from the poetic experience to events which, even if they were part of the initial impetus towards composition, the poet had contrived to dissociate from his lines.

In 1954 my own book *Infinity on the Anvil* came out. This was a fundamentally straightforward commentary on the poetry, as poetry, without reference to side issues of biography, mysticism, dogma or philosophy. As such it was new, and dealt at length with both the short poems and the Lambeth Books. The major books that have come out in the last ten years are named in the Reading List.

Only within the last decade has any of Blake's poetry, including *Songs of Innocence and of Experience*, become available in editions intelligibly or adequately annotated. Earlier the notes were invariably either erudite and critically irrelevant, or casual and of little help.

Further Reading

SELECTIONS

Bateson, F. W., ed., *Selected Poems of William Blake* (Barnes & Noble, New York, 1957). Includes complete texts of *Songs of Innocence* and *of Experience*; extracts from *An Island in the Moon*, and *The Marriage of Heaven and Hell*, selected lyrics from *Poetical Sketches* and the *Notebook*, later lyrics and epigrams. Introduction 20 pp., notes 50 pp., index.

Gardner, Stanley, ed., *William Blake: Selected Poems* (Dufour Editions Inc., Chester Springs, Pa., 1964). Includes complete texts of *Songs of Innocence* and *of Experience*, *The Book of Thel*, *A Song of Liberty*, *Visions of the Daughters of Albion* and *Auguries of Innocence*, extracts from *The Book of Urizen*, *The Song of Los*, selected poems from *Poetical Sketches*, the *Notebook* and later lyrics. Introduction 40 pp., notes 52 pp., index.

COMPLETE WORKS

Erdman, David V. and Bloom, Harold, *The Poetry and Prose of William Blake* (Doubleday, New York, 1965). Notes.

Keynes, Geoffrey, *The Complete Works of William Blake* (Random House; New York, 1957).

COMMENTARIES

Erdman, David V., *Blake: Prophet against Empire* (Princeton Univ. Press, Princeton, N.J., 1954). An indispensable book of immense scholarship, in which Blake's writing is related in detail to the political events of his time.

Fyre, Northrop, *Fearful Symmetry* (Beacon Press, Boston, Mass., 1962). A major critical commentary on Blake.

Gilchrist, A., *Life of William Blake* (Haskell House Pubs., New York).

Gillham, D. G., *Blake's Contrary States* (Cambridge University Press, (Cambridge, Mass., 1966). A detailed· commentary on *Songs of Innocence* and *of Experience*.

Bently, G. E., and Nurmi, Martin, K., *A Blake Bibliography* (University of Minnesota, Minneapolis, Minn., 1964), is the standard reference book.

There are many good facsimiles of Blake's illuminated printing in the libraries, and these should be seen if Blake is to be fully appreciated. For Blake's own times *London Life in the XVIII Century* by M. D. George (Harper & Row, New York, 1964) is recommended; and especially the volumes on the areas of St. Mary Lambeth, South Bank, Vauxhall, St. Pancras (4 vols.) and above all St. James Westminster (4 vols.), in the magnificent Survey of London published by the Greater London Council to which I am indebted for many details.

Index